THINKING
WITH

$\mathcal{G}OD$

SERIES ONE

by

FRANCIS P. LE BUFFE, S.J.

Imprimi potest:

Jacobus P. Sweeney, S. J.

Praep. Prov. Neo-Eboracensis

Nihil obstat:

Arthur J. Scanlan, S. T. D.

Censor Librorum

Imprimatur:

Francis J. Spellman, D. D.

Archbishop, New York

New York, July 10, 1945

First printing, August 1946

THINKING *with* GOD

SERIES I

by

FRANCIS P. LeBUFFE, S.J.

}

The QUEEN'S WORK
3742 WEST PINE BOULEVARD
SAINT LOUIS 8, MISSOURI

TABLE OF CONTENTS

TABLE OF CONTENTS—*Continued*

TABLE OF CONTENTS—*Continued*

THINKING WITH GOD

by

FRANCIS P. LE BUFFE, S.J.

PREFACE

This book contains varied, brief, simple meditations for all who wish to pray mentally, whether they be lay folk, priests or Religious.

The one conviction that I have, after years of lecturing on Mental Prayer, is that there is a real need of books that will present this whole matter simply and enticingly. Too often the whole presentation of Mental Prayer is complicated, stilted and unreal. Moreover there is often little variety in our spiritual diet and so it palls on us just as lack of variety in material food nullifies all desire of eating and drinking.

To secure variety, these little meditations are offered in a helter-skelter way much as the entrees or as French pastry are served in a restaurant. You pick and choose. Christmas thoughts can be as enticing in June as in December, and I dislike labeling a meditation "For Christmas" as though it might not be used at any other time.

Then too these meditations are brief, but I hope, compact with thought. They are mental accordions to be compressed or extended as we have time or God's inspiration moves us.

Finally they are simple, molded according to one of the easiest forms of Mental Prayer, known and used down through the centuries, a form to which St. Ignatius of Loyola attached the name "Second Method of Prayer":

"We can hardly improve on the Saint's own description of this easy form of meditation: 'The person kneeling or seated, according to the greater disposition in which he finds himself and as more devotion accompanies him ... says Father and continues to think over this word so long as he finds meanings, comparisons, relish and consolation in considerations pertaining to this word. And let him act in the same way with each word of the Our Father, or of any other prayers which he wants to say in this way.' The mechanical setup that will be used in these brief meditations, tries to add an extra bit of help. Each thought is suggested and is then followed by three dots, thus ... This is to indicate that the one meditating is to dwell on the thought suggested and should try to develop it. When the thought no longer holds the one meditating or if it fails to appeal at all, then and only then should he pass on to the next thought. Hence these lines are not to be read one after the other rapidly. They are 'chunks of thought' and need to be broken open by the prayerful thinking of the meditator."

Lastly and very importantly we must "let our hearts go as we pray." Hence a "colloquy" or informal chat with Our Lord ends each meditation. We should *always* end thus, informally and freely expressing our inmost thoughts. Of course it would be well to "let our hearts go" *within* the period of meditation, chatting with God if and when and as we please.

For further development of the thoughts suggested in this Preface, I beg leave to refer the reader to my "Let's Try Mental Prayer," published by The Queen's Work.

May this little book put souls more at ease with God. And if it does, won't each say a prayer for the writer, please?

FRANCIS P. LeBUFFE, S. J.

St. Ignatius Church, New York City
Quadragesima Sunday, 1946

CHRIST DWELLS WITH US

The Word was made flesh, and dwelt among us.
—John 1:14

The Word—

    existing from all eternity ...

    born of the Father, yet equal to Him ...

    from whom, as from the Father, proceeds the Holy Ghost ...

    who, with the Father and the Holy Ghost, drew out of noth-
ingness—

        the angels ...

        the sun and moon, earth and stars ...

        the fishes of the sea ...

        the birds of the air ...

        the beasts that roam field and forest ...

        man himself ...

    who, when Adam and Eve sinned, was willing to come to save
them ...

Was made flesh—

    though God, He became a human being just like the rest of
us ...

    He chose Mary, the maid of Galilee, for His Virgin Mother ...

    He chose Joseph as His foster father ...

    He was born in a stable ...

    and was laid in a manger ...

    even from His birth it was true that "the Son of man hath not
where to lay His head" *(Matt. 8:20)* ...

And dwelt among us—

    in His visible life on earth—

        as a helpless child for years ...

        through all the playtime of boyhood ...

        helping Mary with the housework ...

        working with Joseph in his carpentershop ...

        preaching up and down Judea and Galilee ...

        —until men caught Him and crucified Him ...

in His Eucharistic life—

    offering Himself daily in the Mass through the ministry of thousands of priests everywhere ...

    coming to us in Holy Communion to be "our daily bread" ...

    remaining in the Tabernacle—

        to be ready to come to us when we need Him in death ...

        to be visited by us, if we think that much of Him ...

in His Mystical Body—

    where He and we form one mysterious whole ...

    wherein we are united to each other in "the Communion of Saints" ...

    and it is His desire to dwell within each one of us, in mind and heart during this sacred Christmastide ...

Dear Jesus, sweet Babe of Bethlehem, You have been very good to come and dwell among us. None of us deserved that You should become Man to save us; none of us deserved that You should stay with us in the Blessed Sacrament; none of us deserved that You should make us all one with You in the Blessed Sacrament. But You did come. And now I ask You— please come and dwell within me always, in my mind and in my heart. Then I shall daily grow to be more like You. And that is what I really want.

CHRIST'S ABIDING PRESENCE

Thou, O Lord, art among us, and thy name is called upon by us; forsake us not.—Jer. 14:9.

(Used as the Small Chapter of Compline.)

Thou, O Lord, art among us—

    by reason of His omnipresence ...

    because we are members of His Mystical Body ...

    because we are indwelt by the Holy Ghost ...

    because He is present in our Tabernacles ...

    because He is actually present in us after Holy Communion ...

because, we sincerely trust, His ideals reign in our minds and hearts . . .

Thy name is called upon by us—

> privately—
>> in our morning and evening prayers . . .
>> in our grace before and after meals . . .
>> in our frequent acts of aspiration . . .
>> in our visits to Him in the Blessed Sacrament . . .
> publicly—
>> in our prayers before and after class . . .
>> at our Sodality meetings . . .
>> when we say the Angelus in common . . .
>> at Benediction . . .
>> above all at Mass—
>>> when He Himself again becomes the Victim satisfying for our sins . . .
>>> when we unite ourselves with Him in Holy Communion as part of the Sacrifice . . .

Forsake us not—

> when we are young, for then we need His guidance much . . .
> in our youth, for then His wisdom must direct our steps aright . . .
> in older years, that we may handle life's problems properly . . .
> in times of joy, that pleasure may not lead us away from him . . .
> in times of sadness, that we may not grow depressed . . .
> when we have sinned, that we may remember His mercy . . .
> at the hour of our death, that He may take us *home* . . .

Dear Jesus, You are my God and my Creator, and I turn my heart longingly to You. You have been very good to me, but I have repaid You shabbily. I am sorry for my meannesses; and I am glad that despite it all, I am still Yours, and You want me to be Yours forever. Despite it all, You are with me always and everywhere. Thank You so much for that. Please don't ever leave me alone by myself.

FOR CHRIST'S LOVE

For the charity of Christ presseth us.—2 Cor. 5:14

The charity of Christ—

   Christ's love for me—

      by which He created me ...

      through which He continually guides me ...

      which led Him to become Man for me ...

      which moved Him to die for me ...

      which keeps Him a prisoner on our altars ...

      which brings Him into our bodies in Holy Communion ...

      which makes us one with Him in His Mystical Body ...

      which is always the same, no matter what I am ...

   my love for Christ—

      in return for my existence ...

      in appreciation of His Providence ...

      aroused by His choice of me to be a Catholic ...

      increased by His constant gift of grace ...

      based on—

         His goodness to me ...

         His own goodness in Himself ...

      but my love is fickle and sometimes very cold ...

      yet fundamentally I do want to love Him ...

      and His love is never really dead within me ...

Presseth us—

   filling our minds with the thought of Him ...

   warming our hearts in His service ...

   nerving our wills to do and dare for Him ...

Presseth us—

   at home, that His peace may reign there ...

   in school, that we may learn more about Him ...

   at play, that we may win His approval then ...

   at work, that we may sanctify our toil as He did His ...

Presseth us—

   when we are with the pagan-minded ...

   when we are with non-Catholic companions ...

when we are with lax Catholics . . .
when we are with fervent Catholics . . .
that always and everywhere we may be "the good odour of
· Christ" *(2 Cor. 2:15)* . . .

Dear Jesus, I do love You, maybe in a fickle way, but still deep down in my heart I do love You. That is fine. But better still You love me. And because You love me I want to do something, no, I want to do very much, in return. So let Your love press me forward and drive me on to do and dare not only great things for You, but the hard little things of everyday life.

SEEING CHRIST'S GLORY

Today you shall know that the Lord will come and in the morning you shall see his glory.—Introit of the Mass of the Vigil of Christmas, Based on Exodus 16: 6, 7. (Moses spoke thus to the Israelites in the desert, promising them food in their hunger.)

Today—

on Christmas Eve when we are all expecting Our Lord . . .
after the four-weeks' preparation of Advent . . .
and shall I have prepared myself the way I should—
by extra prayers? . . .
by extra little penances? . . .
by more frequent and more fervent Communion? . . .
every day of every week of every month of every year? . . .

Today—

when the world is filled with hate and the dreadful aftermath
of war . . .
when so much of normal life is gone . . .
when perhaps we ourselves are anxious and worried . . .

You shall know—

through the eyes of faith . . .
through the touching liturgy of the Church . . .

That the Lord will come—

not in majesty or in pomp . . .
not in the thunders and lightnings of Sinai . . .
but humbly—
    as a Babe . . .
    in a stable . . .
    in a manger . . .
    with a Mother and foster father who seem quite ordinary . . .
unobtrusively, making so little stir in His creation . . .
lovingly . . .
appealingly . . .

And in the morning you shall see His glory—

the glory of a tiny Babe, "omnipotence in bonds" . . .
the glory of a Virgin Mother . . .
the glory of the angels singing on the hills . . .
the glory of the lowly shepherds' adoration . . .
and now the glory of the triple Mass—
    the first, in honor of His eternal birth . . .
    the second, for His birth at Bethlehem . . .
    the third, for His birth in our own hearts . . .
the strange glory of the tiny white Host . . .
the stranger glory of being my guest within my own body . . .
the strangest glory the world has ever seen . . .

Dear Jesus, You know how I love Christmas and You in the Christmas mysteries. You seem very close to me then: helpless, just as I; poor, just as I; one of the crowd, just as I. Yet all the while You are God. You were very good to become just like me. Please give me much grace to become just like You.

AS WE COME AND GO

May the Lord keep thy coming in and thy going out; from henceforth now and for ever.—Ps. 120:8

May the Lord—

in His power . . .
in His wisdom . . .

in His mercy..
in His Providence...
in His love...

Keep thy coming in—

as the New Year breaks in upon us...
as each day begins...
as each task arises...
as each pleasure offers itself...
as we enter our homes...
as we report for work...

And thy going out—

as the Old Year ends...
as each night falls...
as each task is fulfilled...
as each burden is laid aside...
as we part from our loved ones...
as we leave chance acquaintances...
as life itself filters out to the last moment...

From henceforth now—

in youth, when the tide of life runs high...
in mature life, when graver problems confront us...
in declining years, when we are nearing home...
when we are with those who know not God...
when dealing with those who dislike God's ways...
when our friends are the friends of God too...

And for ever—

throughout eternity...
as we companion with the saints...
and enjoy Our Blessed Mother's company...
before the unveiled vision of the Father, Son and Holy
    Ghost...

Dear Jesus, as the New Year breaks in upon me, I ask You
to keep me safe throughout its every day and hour. Keep my

coming in and my going out, always and everywhere. And, if You call me before another New Year comes, please see me safely home.

FOR GOD'S OWN SAKE

Arise, O Lord, help us and redeem us for Thy name's sake.—Ps. 43:26

Arise, O Lord—

not that God does not know our needs ...

not that He is unmindful of us ...

not that He is unwilling to help us ...

but because He has ordained that we should pray to Him ...

and because it is natural for the creature to cry unto his Creator ...

and because children are wont to call on father in times of distress ...

Help us—

help us in body—

that our passions may not blind us ...

that our feelings may not rule us ...

that in health we may serve You aright ...

that in sickness we may be resigned ...

help us in soul—

that error may not mislead our minds ...

that sin may not swerve our wills ...

that sin may be increasingly distasteful ...

that virtue may be increasingly attractive ...

Redeem us for Thy name's sake—

we do not deserve it ...

our claim is upon Your mercy ...

and yet more, "for Thy name's sake"—

for we are Your creatures, and You must not lose us ...

for we are Your children, and You want us with You ...

for we are redeemed by Your Precious Blood, and You

must not be cheated of what you bought . . .

for we are Your living temples, and Your tabernacles
should not be polluted and ruined . . .

we say it reverently: You owe it to Your good name to see
that we are saved.

Dear Lord, I need Your help. You know it and I know it. I have no least claim upon Your mercy or Your help because of anything I have done. But I am Your creature and I am Your child. So for Your own name's sake help me and see me safely home.

GOD'S MERCY BE ON US

May God have mercy on us, and bless us: may He cause the light of His countenance to shine upon us, and may He have mercy on us.—Ps. 66:2

May God have mercy on us—

because we are slow-footed in goodness . . .
because we are quick to sin . . .
because we are inconstant . . .

And bless us—

in the morning, when we awaken . . .
during the day, while we perform the tasks of life . . .
in our hours of leisure, that we may pass them holily . . .
at night, when we rebuild our strength for another day . . .
in youth, that we may pass it wisely . . .
in the middle years, that we may handle life's problems
aright . . .
in the grave-ward years, to buoy up our faltering steps . . .

**May he cause the light of His countenance to shine
upon us—**

that our minds may be enlightened to see the truth . . .
that our wills may be strengthened to do the good . . .
that our memory may recall what is profitable to holy living . . .
that we may see the world and all that is in it as He sees it . . .

And may He have mercy on us—

  because He is our Father...

  because He is our Redeemer...

  because He is our Sanctifier...

  because without His forgiveness we are lost...

  because He wants us home with Him...

  because we, too, want to be home with Him, unendingly...

  Dear Lord, I need You and need You badly. Sin attracts me much at times, and holy living often seems very unattractive. But I must "make good" and come home to Heaven where You and I both want me to be. So help me to see and to do what is right—always and everywhere.

HIS RESURRECTION OUR HOPE

The Lord has risen from the grave, alleluia,
Who had hung for us on the tree, alleluia,
　　　　　　　　—Versicle and Response for Easter

The Lord has risen from the grave—

  "Whom God hath raised up, having loosed the sorrows of hell, as it was impossible that He should be holden by it" (Acts. 2:24)...

  "He was crucified, died, and was buried; the third day He rose again from the dead" (Creed)...

  the "first death," the death of the body, still remains for us; but the "second death," the eternal death of the soul, has been vanquished by His death...

  for by His death Heaven is opened to us...

  and all the joys of the Beatific Vision are ours—if we want them...

Alleluia (Praise ye the Lord)—

  yes, praise Him because the night of sin is gone...

  yes, praise Him because death has been robbed of its terrors...

  yes, praise Him because the door of our heavenly home has been opened...

• 14 •

Who had hung for us on the tree—

dying the death of utmost shame . . .

dying between two thieves . . .

dying as the outcast, rejected king of His own people . . .

dying for us and for our sins . . .

for "He was wounded for our iniquities, He was bruised for our sins . . . and by His bruises we are healed" *(Isa. 53:5)* . . .

Alleluia (Praise ye the Lord)—

yes, praise Him—

because He "hath redeemed us from the curse of the law" *(Gal. 3:13)* . . .

because He has shown us how to bear our trials, being "led as a sheep to the slaughter" *(Isa. 53:7)* . . .

because He has shown us how victory can come out of utter defeat . . .

because His Resurrection after His cruel death proves that "the sufferings of this time are not worthy to be compared to the glory to come" *(Rom. 8:18)* . . .

yes, praise Him "from now and unto eternity" . . .

Dear Jesus, risen out of love for me, You have given me much courage to put up with the trials of life. Life does become hard at times, and I get very tired of fighting and struggling against unending odds. But Your Resurrection makes life different and makes the struggle worth while. So give me grace to fight ahead, that one day I may rise glorious with You.

PLEASE UNDERSTAND ME!

Give ear, O Lord, to my words!
    Understand my cry.
Hearken to the voice of my prayer,
    O my King and my God.
                                   —Ps. 5:2, 3

Give ear, O Lord, to my words—

God knows my least needs, better even than I do myself...

yet as a loving Father, He wants me, His child, to ask His help...

still I realize my unworthiness...

and I fear my past sins may even offset His mercy...

and so I pray to Him to "give ear to my words"...

Understand my cry—

sometimes my prayer is definite and clear-cut...

sometimes I am very vague as to my own wants...

and, even when I know my needs, I often do not know what will help best...

sometimes my heart is so cold and my soul so dry, I can but murmur inarticulately...

sometimes my prayer is just a routine mumble...

Hearken to the voice of my prayer—

I stand in need of mercy, and yet I do not deserve it...

yet my cry is the cry of an humble suppliant...

and it is full of confidence, for He is "my King and my God"...

O my King and my God—

He has created me out of nothing...

He has redeemed me in His blood...

He has sanctified me by His indwelling...

all that I have and all that I am is His...

and so I have a claim on Him...

and He recognizes and will act on that claim...

"hear my prayer"—

the pleading of child with Father...

the suppliance of subject with King...

the prayer of creature to God...

O my God, I need You much. Without Your sustaining Omnipotence I would drop back into nothingness. I need Your grace to solve the problems of life and to avoid its pitfalls. And so I come to You my Father and ask You to help me Your child. Understand my cry, even when I do not understand it myself. Father, help me even when I pray in routine fashion. Understand, please understand, my cry.

PROOF OF CHRIST'S LOVE

Wherefore Jesus also, that He might sanctify the people by His own blood, suffered without the gate.—Heb. 13:12. Used as Response on the Feast of the Most Precious Blood.

Wherefore Jesus also—

> just as the sacrifices were offered in the Old Law, so Our Lord was sacrificed in the New...
> but those sacrifices were repeated; He died but once...

That He might sanctify—

> restoring to them the grace Adam had lost...
> and when they had lost this once more through personal sin, giving it back again...
> the one purpose of His life was to sanctify and save...

The People—

> not men of one race or of one clime or of one age...
> but Jew and Gentile, bond and free...
> from the beginning of the world unto the end of time...

By His own blood—

> He gave not His possessions but Himself for us...
> and He did it knowingly and most willingly...
> and He did it because He loved us...

Suffered without the gate—

> even as "the bodies of those beasts whose blood is brought into the holies by the High Priest for sin, are burned without the camp" (Heb. 13:11)...
> even as criminals were taken outside the city to be put to death...

and all this He did to turn me away from sin and to win
my love . . .

Dear Jesus, I thank You for Your love for me, love so great
that it caused You to die the most horrible and most shameful
of deaths. Let me always remember Your love and let that memory hold my heart far away from every least sin and keep my
soul in every way and for ever Yours.

GOD IS MY REWARD

**Fear not, Abram, I am thy protector, and thy
reward exceeding great.—Gen. 15:1**

Fear not, Abram—
> God's usual greeting to men was "fear not" . . .
> for He is our loving Father . . .
> and He always wants to help us . . .
> and it is only when we will not let Him, that He does not
> help us . . .
> my attitude to God should always be one of loving trust . . .
> Abram's was, and for that God changed his name to Abraham,
> "father of many nations" *(Gen. 17:5)* . . .
> is that my attitude toward God? . . .

I am thy protector—
> surely He was a protector all during Abraham's long life . . .
> though He tried Abraham in many ways . . .
> and He is and always will be my protector—
>> when I am young, to teach me the ways of virtue . . .
>> when I am mature, to help me solve life's tangles . . .
>> when I am old, to steady my steps to Heaven . . .
> my protector—
>> in time of want . . .
>> in hours of doubt . . .
>> when temptations are strong . . .

Thy reward exceeding great—
> to Abraham God promised—
>> a child in his old age . . .

• 18 •

the land of Palestine as his heritage ...

descendants as numberless as the stars of the heavens ...
to us God promises—

His sanctifying grace and His love ...

Himself—

in this life, by His indwelling in our souls ...

in the next life, when we are to be happy with Him
for all eternity ...

O my God, truly You are my protector and my reward
exceeding great. To Abraham You gave many blessings, but You
give many, many more to me. He did not have You in the
Mass, in Holy Communion, always present on the altar. You
did not give him Mary as his Mother. I thank You, yes, I thank
You from my heart for all You have done for me. Just make
me worthy of it all.

REST FOR OUR DEAD

**To all who rest in Christ, grant, we beseech Thee,
a place of refreshment, of light and of peace.**

—From the Commemoration of the Dead in the Canon.

To all who rest in Christ—

living, they have confessed Christ on their lips and by their
actions ...

they have died in the true faith as members of His mystical
Body ...

"blessed are the dead who die in the Lord. From henceforth
now, saith the Spirit, that they may rest from their
labours" *(Apoc. 14:13)* ...

Grant we beseech Thee—

they can no longer help themselves ...

from us alone can succor come to them ...

and so we lift our hands and hearts in prayer ...

A place of refreshment—

> after the weariness of life...
> after earning their bread in the sweat of their brows...
> after bearing the burdens and heat of the day...

A place of light—

> after their pilgrimage through the valley of tears...
> after they have left those "who sit in darkness, and in the shadow of death" (Luke 1:79)...
> after the doubts and misgivings which so often clouded their minds...

A place of peace—

> after the strife and friction of life...
> after the misunderstanding with even those they loved...
> after the struggle between virtue and sin within their own hearts...

A place of refreshment, of light and peace—

> which means being at home with God forever...
> and with Christ their elder Brother...
> and with Mary their Mother...
> and with all the saints that have come home before them...

Dear Jesus, be mindful of these holy dead. You died for them; and You want them with You now. But You have made their homecoming dependent on the help that we give them. So I shall pray for them and offer up my good works for them. And I hope, when I too come home to You, that I shall have sent many of them home to You ahead of me.

A YEAR OF OUR LORD

The year of the Lord, 1946 (or any year).

The year—

> 365 days wherein to work, 365 nights wherein to rest...
> 365 long opportunities for good, 365 long opportunities for evil...

365 days and nights—

of God's conserving me away from nothingness...
of God's Providence and guidance...
another year of day's brilliance and of night's bright galaxies of stars...
another year of sunshine and of rain...
another year of evil men's plottings...
another year of good men's strivings...

Of the Lord—

another year since the birth of Christ at Bethlehem...
another year since He died on the Cross...
another year since He formed His Mystical Body, the Church...
another year of manifold actual graces...
another year of lavish sanctifying grace—

through my prayers and good works...
through the sacramentals...
through the Mass...
through the Sacraments...
one year nearer Heaven...
one year closer to Father's home...

1946 (or any year)—

for some the first year of life, for some the last...
for some a year of success, for some a year of disappointments...
for some a year of health, for some a slow-footed year of pain...
for some a year of happiness, for some a lengthening way of the Cross...
but for all "a year of the Lord"—

given graciously by Him...
blessed bountifully by Him...
enriched with His gifts of nature and of grace...
—and it lies within my power to form and fashion it for Him...

Dear Jesus, I accept this New Year from Your hands. It may be my last and next New Year's day I may celebrate with You. But whether it be my last or not, I want it to be *Your* year, I want each month, each day, each hour, each minute to be *Yours*. So give me much grace to make this year truly "a year of the Lord."

HIS PEACE BE TO US

Grace unto you, and peace from God Our Father, and from the Lord Jesus Christ.—2 Thess. 1:2.

Usual Salutation of St. Paul in His Epistles.

Grace—
> that supernatural life which God gave to Adam but which he lost deliberately . . .
> that supernatural life which Jesus Christ won back for us . . .
> sanctifying grace—
>> which blots out mortal sin . . .
>> which makes us like to God . . .
>> by which we become children of God and heirs of Heaven . . .
>> which brings with it the indwelling of the Holy Ghost . . .

Peace—
> in our own minds, which are so often led astray by error . . .
> in our own hearts, which so often love wrongly . . .
> in our own wills, which so easily yield to temptation . . .
> peace between friends . . .
> peace between enemies . . .
> peace between God and man . . .

From God our Father—
> who created us . . .
> who formed us to His own image and likeness . . .
> who sustains us in existence . . .
> who wants us to have this grace and peace so that we may be with Him in Heaven forever . . .

And from the Lord Jesus Christ—

"who being in the form of God ... emptied Himself, taking
the form of a servant" *(Phil. 2:6, 7)* ...

"who for us men and for our salvation descended from
Heaven and became incarnate" *(Creed)* ...

who "having loved His own who were in the world, He loved
them unto the end" *(John 13:1)* ...

"by His bruises we are healed" *(Isa. 53:5)* ...

by whose Redemption we have received "grace for grace"
(John 1:16) ...

who said: "Peace I leave with you, my peace I give unto
you" *(John 14:27)* ...

Dear Jesus, give me plentifully of Your grace and peace.
Life on earth has always been hard for man since he lost his first
innocence, and it is doubly hard now. You Yourself said that
the road home to You is straight and narrow. So please make
it a bit easier by Your grace and peace.

BLOT OUT MY INIQUITY!

**Have mercy on me, O God, according to Thy great
mercy. And according to the multitude of Thy
tender mercies blot out my iniquity.—Ps. 50:3**

Have mercy, O God—

we are always in need of God's mercy ...

we always stand in need of His patience and long suffering ...

for we are built of flesh and blood and are heirs to many
frailties ...

and often we knowingly and deliberately offend Him ...

On me—

"of all man's clotted clay the dingiest clot" ...

knowing my weaknesses, yet not standing sufficiently on
guard against them ...

realizing the occasions of my sins, yet not avoiding them as
I should ...

According to Thy great mercy—

God is just, but "His tender mercies are over all His works" (Ps. 144:9) . . .

God is wise, and so He knows how to see the good within us . .

God is all-powerful, and so He can afford to be lenient on us . . .

And according to the multitude of Thy tender mercies—

shown to Adam and Eve, when they had rebelled . . .

shown to the Jews, when they fell into idolatry at the foot of Mount Sinai . . .

shown to David, after his adultery and murder . . .

shown to Peter, when he had denied his Master . . .

shown to Magdalen, after her life of sin . . .

shown to me, every time God pardoned my sins . . .

Blot out my iniquity—

my sins of thought and word and deed . . .

my serious sins . . .

my lesser sins . . .

my sins of malice . . .

my sins of weakness . . .

—and only an infinitely merciful God could forgive so much . . .

Dear Jesus, there is much in my life that has offended You. I am sorry for it all. Some of it was wilful, some came from weakness. But I am sorry now and I humbly ask Your pardon; and I know You will forgive me and forget, because of all Your tender mercies.

TURNING GOD OUT OF DOORS

O expectation of Israel, the Saviour thereof in time of trouble: why wilt thou be as a stranger in the land, and as a wayfaring man turning in to lodge?—Jer. 14:8

O expectation of Israel—

    to the Jews of old God was their "expectation"—

        foretold by patriarch and prophet . . .

        longed for by every true child of Israel . . .

        yet forgotten time and again by them . . .

    to Catholics of today, God is our "expectation"—

        because we acknowledge and honor Him as our one, true God . . .

        because we accept His Church as the one, true Church . . .

    and yet we have frequently acted like the Jews of old . . .

The Saviour thereof in time of trouble—

    time and again the Jews were saved by God . . .

    time and again God has come visibly to the aid of His Church . . .

    time and again in each of our lives we have been delivered from our trials by Him . . .

Why wilt thou be as a stranger in the land—

    read the history of the Jews and see how often they rejected God . .

    read the history of the Church and see how whole nations have left God . . .

    look at the world today—

        the lands of the Orient, where God is indeed a stranger . . .

        Russia, where men give their lives to drive Him out of the lives of other men . . .

        Germany, where men have defied Him and His laws . . .

        in even so-called Christian countries, where men have quite forgotten Him and His ideals . . .

        even among Catholics—how many really welcome God into their hearts and into their lives? . . .

As a wayfaring man turning in to lodge—

    "He came unto His own, and His own received Him not" (*John 1:11*) . . .

    "There was no room for them in the inn" (*Luke 2:7*) . . .

    God looking for a place to lodge! . . .

God like a homeless man! ...
that is the story in so many places today ...
is it the story of my heart? ..

My God, if You were less than God, You would be discouraged, and dare I say it, bitter against mankind which You have made. After all You have done for us, we have turned You out of doors—and tried to run the world without You. And even in my own heart, I haven't welcomed You any too decently. That ought not to be, because I know Your love better than most men. Forgive my rudeness in the past and please give me much grace never to turn You out of doors from my heart again.

WAIT FOR THE LORD

Expect the Lord! Do manfully! And let thy heart take courage. And wait thou for the Lord.—Ps. 26:14

Expect the Lord—
>   we poor human beings are always in a hurry ...
>   because we know our days are few and numbered ...
>   and we find it hard to wait at all ...
>   and very hard to wait on God—
>>   for we know our needs ...
>>   and we know His power ...
>>   and we want Him to use that power now ...
>   yet for reasons He knows best God often makes us wait ...

Do manfully—
>   fixing our minds in the knowledge of what is right ...
>   schooling our will in doing what is right ...
>   relying on God's grace to fight ahead ...
>   "I can do all things in Him who strengtheneth me" *(Phil. 4:13)* ..

And let thy heart take courage—
>   as Abraham's did when told to sacrifice Isaac ...
>   as Judith's did when she slew Holofernes ...

as Esther's did when she saved Israel...

as Moses' did when he dared combat Pharoah...

as Peter's did when he defied the High Priest and continued
to preach Christ...

as did and does the heart of every saint who fights the battles
of God...

as the heart of Mother Mary did when she accepted the
motherhood of God...

as did the Heart of Christ throughout His Passion...

And wait thou for the Lord—

no matter how dark the hour may be...

no matter how sharp the pain may be...

no matter how heavy the cross may be...

no matter how unjustly men may treat me...

no matter how far God may seem to be away...

"as the shepherd visiteth his flock—so will I visit my sheep,
and will deliver them out of all the places where they
have been scattered in the cloudy and dark day"
(Ezech. 34:12)...

Dear Lord, at times life grows very dark and the tasks of life
seem all too burdensome, and worst of all, You seem very, very
far away, when I need You most. I do want to fight the fight
of life aright and I don't want to fail You. So let me be strong
and let my heart be always filled with courage; waiting for You
as long as You want me to wait, knowing all the while that You
are silently, powerfully helping me.

OUR CLAIM ON GOD'S AID

**Give aid therefore, we beseech Thee, to Thy
servants whom Thou hast redeemed by Thy
Precious Blood.**—Verse From the Te Deum

Give aid—

to us "poor banished children of Eve"...

to us who of ourselves are weak, and fickle too...

aid to our bodies—

that we enjoy good health ...

that we obtain proper livelihood ...

aid to our souls—

that we may avoid all sin ...

that we may perform our duties well ...

that we may attain great holiness ...

To Thy servants—

by our very nature, we are creatures of God ...

thus by our very nature we belong to God—

at all times ...

in all places ..

in all things ...

yet now we are more than servants, yes, dearly loved sons ...

Whom Thou hast redeemed by Thy Precious Blood—

we had sinned, but God did not forsake us ...

but even in the Garden of Eden God promised our redemption ...

and when "the fulness of time" had come, the God-Man shed His Precious Blood for us—

in the circumcision ...

in the agony ...

when the soldiers scourged Him ...

when they pressed down the cruel crown of thorns ...

when they nailed Him to the Cross ...

when Longinus opened up His side ...

so we are His by every right of creation and redemption ...

and we can claim His aid ...

and He is most anxious to help us always and everywhere ...

Dear Jesus, thanks to Your love, You have redeemed my soul by Your Precious Blood. The greatest consolation of my life is that I belong to You, and that You really want to keep me Yours—always. So help me, please, at all times and in all places to act worthily of You. Then I shall be Yours—always.

GOD'S LATEST MESSAGE TO US

God, who, at sundry times and in divers manners, spoke in times past to the fathers by the prophets, last of all, in these days hath spoken to us by His Son.—Heb. 1:1,2. Used as Epistle for the Third Mass of Christmas.

God, who, at sundry times and in divers manners, spoke in times past to the fathers by the prophets—

He spoke to the fathers—

to Adam, making the first promise of the Redeemer ...

to Noe, saving mankind from utter destruction ...

to Abraham, promising to bless all his descendants ...

to Moses, leading forth His chosen people from bondage ...

to David, who sang so joyfully and so sorrowfully of the future Messias ...

to Isaias and Malachias, Daniel and Micheas, and all the prophets ..

at sundry times and in divers manners—

by the near-sacrifice of Isaac ...

by Melchisedech's bread and wine ...

by the thunders and lightnings of Sinai ...

by the manna in the desert ...

by the cloud presence in the Holy of Holies ...

by the Virgin Mother foretold by Isaias ...

by Daniel's seventy weeks of years ...

by Malachy's clean offering ...

by Micheas' vision of the Messias coming forth from Bethlehem ...

Last of all, in these days hath spoken to us by His Son—

we are the heirs of the ages of God's partial revelations ...

for "when the fulness of the time was come, God sent His

Son, made of a woman, made under the Law" *(Gal. 4:4)* ...

He is truly Emmanuel—"God-with-us"—

in likeness of human nature ...

in the sharing of all our experiences, sin alone excepted ...

in the union of His Mystical Body ...

in His presence on our altars ...

in His indwelling within us after Holy Communion ...

thus Christmas means the culmination of the hopes of ages ...

and it means the tangible nearness of Christ ...

and it means that joy and gratitude should fill our hearts ...

Dear Infant Saviour, if You were not God, I would doubt that You know all that Your coming means to me. Life is hard at times, and the shadows darken and the crosses fall upon me frighteningly. But You have come, and You are with me always. That makes all the difference in the world—and from my heart, here in Your sacramental Presence, I thank You.

TELL MEN ABOUT GOD

How beautiful upon the mountains are the feet of him that bringeth good tidings, and that preacheth peace; of him that showeth forth good, that preacheth salvation, that saith to Sion: Thy God shall reign.—Isa. 52:7

How beautiful upon the mountains are the feet of him that bringeth good tidings—

these words were first spoken by the Prophet Isaias of the fall of the Babylonian monarchy and the return of the Jews from captivity ...

they can be said now of each of us Catholics who bring to a world, captive in sin, the good tidings of Christ ...

and these tidings are the truths of our Catholic faith and the principles of our sound morality ...

there is no one more beautiful before God and man today
than the true Catholic...

And that preacheth peace—

peace within our own families...
peace with our companions...
peace within our beloved country...

Of him that showeth forth good—

by our words...
by our actions..
with those we know and love...
with chance acquaintances...
in our hours of serious work...
especially in our time of merry-making...

That preacheth salvation—

salvation from sin through God's strong grace...
salvation finally in Heaven through God's gift of perse-
verance...
salvation now to a world gone mad, by bringing back God
into men's lives...

That saith to Sion; Thy God shall reign—

as Catholics, we make a special profession of holiness...
and so we, more than all others, must bring God back into
His world...
and we shall do this by showing to all men—
our firm faith in the unseen world around us...
our lively hope of a better life after death...
our all-inclusive charity in a world of hate...
and best of all our *living* our faith at each moment of
life...

Dear Jesus, I promise to do my part to bring Your tidings
of holiness and of peace to each and every one I meet. My
world may be very small and I may be very insignificant; but I
can and want to do my share to bring the world back to You, and
You back into the world. And I know I shall do that best not

by preaching or by talking but by being a good Catholic at all times and in all places. So please give me much grace to *live* my faith—always.

BE MINDFUL OF OUR DEAD

Be mindful also, O Lord, of Thy servants who have gone before us with the sign of faith and sleep the sleep of peace.—Memento of the Dead in the Canon of the Mass

Be mindful also, O Lord of Thy servants—

God is mindful of them...

but He has willed that His mercy towards the Holy Souls will be moved only through our prayers and good works...

and by so doing we fulfill our part in the Communion of Saints...

"and if a brother or sister be naked, and want daily food, and one of you say to them: Go in peace, be ye warmed and filled, yet give them not those things that are necessary for the body, what shall it profit?" (*Jas. 2:15,16*)...

what nakedness and hunger like to that of the Holy Souls!...

Who have gone before us—

they have "gone before" us, and we shall most certainly follow...

"our little systems have their day, they have their day and cease to be"...

"children of a day, what are we, what are we not!"...

might it not then be wise to pray for them, for we too shall need prayers some day?..

With the sign of faith—

with St. Paul each Holy Soul can say: "I have fought a good fight, I have finished my course, I have kept the faith" (*2 Tim. 4:7*)...

"for although he has sinned, he did not deny the Father and the Son and the Holy Ghost, but believed in them" *(Prayers for the Dying)* . . .

they were signed indelibly with "the sign of faith"—
when Baptism made them children of God and heirs of Heaven . . .
when Confirmation made them soldiers of Christ . . .

He "hath sealed us, and given the pledge of the Spirit in our hearts" *(2 Cor. 1:22)* . . .

And sleep the sleep of peace—

dying in grace, they have avoided the "second death" which means eternal privation of the life of God . . .

and so their "first death," that of the body, is only a sleep, from which they will be awakened . . .

that is why we Catholics call the graveyard *cemetery,* which means sleeping place . . .

the Holy Souls are at peace, but greater peace will be theirs when they come *home* to God . . .

and we—only we—can speed that homecoming . . .

Dear Jesus, it is the law of Your love that we who are still journeying homewards, should help the Holy Souls by our prayers and good works. Don't let us be selfish and thoughtless, leaving them in exile, longing to be with You. But give us much grace to be mindful of them always, especially during the month of the Holy Souls.

COME, LET US ADORE HIM!

Christ is born for us. Come, let us adore Him.
—Inviatory at Matins for Christmas

Christ—

from all eternity—
the Second Person of the Most Blessed Trinity . . .
the eternal Son of the Father . . .

from whom, as well as from the Father, proceeds the Holy Ghost...

with no beginning and with no end...

in time—

Mary's Son, and her only one...

descending from Heaven to clothe Himself with our flesh...

Is born for us—

a helpless Babe...

hiding His Godhead behind His humanity...

in a stable, for want of a better place to be born...

wrapped in swaddling clothes, for want of better garments...

laid in a manger, for want of a better bed...

yet heralded by angels...

and adored by shepherds and the Magi...

Come, let us adore Him—

He has come to save me...

He has come to win my love..

from the manger His way of life will be a hard one right up to the Cross...

and all will be out of love for me...

surely I should adore Him—

in my mind, acknowledging Him to be God...

with my lips, trying to make men know Him...

by my actions, that from them men may know that I love Him...

in my heart, where He should be enthroned as complete Lord and King of my life...

Come, let us adore Him—

reverently...

lovingly..

joyfully...

—and always...

Dear Infant Jesus, I adore You in the manger. It was very good of You to come down from Heaven for me. You could

• 34 •

have stayed up there and left me to fight my way in a world darkened by Adam's sin. But You loved me too much for that, and from my heart I thank You for Your love. Just help me to be a bit more worthy of it.

DUST, YES, BUT—!

Remember, man, that thou art dust, and unto dust thou shalt return.—Said at the Distribution of the Ashes on Ash Wednesday

Remember—

when the tide of life is running strong in youth . . .
when the tide of life is at its full in maturer years . . .
when the tide of life begins to ebb in old age . . .

Remember—

when success crowns your efforts . . .
when failure saps your energy . . .
when the colorless routine of life irks you . . .

Remember—

for by nature you forget very easily . . .
and everything round about you tends to distract you . . .

That thou are dust—

you seem to be so strong . . .
you seem to be so self-sufficient . . .
you are so fair and comely to behold . . .
but "dust thou art"—

and so easily stricken with disease . . .
and so easily crushed with a blow . . .
and so easily and utterly broken in an accident . . .
and so helpless to ward off harm . . .
"compost of heaven and mire . . . a thing of whim and wavering" . . .

And unto dust thou shalt return—

today so strong, tomorrow helpless on a bed of pain...
today walking with all the pride of life, tomorrow cold and stilled in death...
today going whithersoever you want, tomorrow tucked deep into a narrow grave...

And unto dust thou shalt return—

mortal in your body, but immortal in your soul...
frail and weak, but all the same only a little less than the angels...
and all the while the child of God...
and every moment the tabernacle of the Holy Spirit...
and so the grave holds no terror, for it is only the shallow vestibule of Heaven...
and death is merely the short, dark tunnel that leads into the blazing glory of God's throne...
dust, yes, but dust that is splendor...

Dear Lord, I sometimes feel very proud and self-sufficient, and it is good that You remind me that I am dust and shall return to dust. It helps to keep my foolish head from being turned. Then, too, You have been good enough to let me know how much You value my soul and that I mean a lot to You. So please give me grace to live in such a way that, when my body turns to dust, my soul may go straight home to You.

TRUE PENANCE

Rend your hearts, and not your garments, and turn to the Lord your God! for He is gracious and merciful.—Joel 2:13. Used as the Responsory in the Office of the First Sunday of Lent.

Rend your hearts, and not your garments—

the purpose of Lent is not penance and self-denial just in and for themselves...

but conquest of self, the "rending of the heart" . . .

we have sinned and yielded to unruly tendencies . . .

now we must look in on our souls and try to make all good again . . .

we have been disobedient; now we shall obey readily . . .

we have been lazy; now we shall do each job most perfectly . . .

we have been vain and proud; now we shall check this silliness . . .

we have prayed listlessly; now we shall pray politely . . .

we have thought but little of God; these holy days we shall try to keep very near Him . . .

and all the little penances will be done to help us reform ourselves . . .

And turn to the Lord your God—

we belong to Him . . .

He wants us . . .

and, deep down in our hearts, we want Him . . .

but we have strayed from Him by our sins . . .

and we have not been very mindful of His love . . .

and so we shall try to be more in love with Him each day of Lent . . .

Because He is gracious and merciful—

Lent is not gloomy, for God is kind . . .

nor is Lent a time of sadness, since God is merciful . . .

and all through her liturgy the Church insists on this spirit of trust and hope . . .

our sins are bad, and many—but God is gracious . . .

we have been rebellious—but God is Our Father . . .

and so from our sins we turn to Him with utter trust . . .

Dear God, I have sinned and been very forgetful of Your love. But I am sorry for it now and I'll do my little Lenten penances with a smile. They are just a token of my love for You, and of my sorrow for the past. I know You will forgive me and that is why there will be no gloom in my Lent, but a holy joy because through Your grace my sins will be forgiven and I shall grow daily in Your love. Please grant that it be so.

HE IS STILL WITH ME

I rose up and am still with thee. Alleluia.
—Ps. 138:18. Used as the Introit of Easter.

I rose up—

> I died for you ...
> and I died the most horrible form of death known to man ...
> and I lay in the tomb, cold and dead, for you ...

I rose up—

> my soul came back to my Body and made it live again ...
> and I passed through the solid rock of the grave ...
> and I paid my first risen visit to my own dear Mother ...
> and then I met Peter, and Mary Magdalen, and all the Apostles ...
> for forty days I stayed away from Heaven to strengthen and console them ...

And am still with thee—

> I promised the Apostles not to leave them orphans ...
> and so I am with you still—
> > in my Church, which is my Mystical Body ...
> > in the Blessed Sacrament, which is I ...
> > by my indwelling in your soul, which is my temple ...
> > by my holy inspirations ...
> > by my guidance and protection of your every action—if you want it so ...

And am still with thee—

> are you equally interested in Me? ...
> are you with Me—
> > in thought? ...
> > in word? ...
> > in deed? ...
> do you really love Me as much as you could? ...

Alleluia (Praise be to God)—

yes, for all His goodness to all men and to me in particular ...
yes, too, for the fact that I still really love Him ...

Dear Jesus, how glad I am that You rose from the dead and much gladder that You are with us still, even to the end of time. I have not shown my gratitude the way I should but I promise to do better from now on. You are with me, and I want to be with You always—in thought and word and deed. Please keep me near You always!

SHALL I KINDLE HIS FIRE?

I am come to cast fire on the earth: and what will I, but that it be kindled?—Luke 12:49

I am come to cast fire on the earth—

the fire of God's love had been quenched when Adam and Eve sinned

but God relighted it in their hearts by His forgiveness ...

yet again their children and their children's children forgot God more and more ...

and their forgetfulness was so complete that He sent the deluge to destroy them ...

even His chosen people forgot Him time and time again ...

but all the time, through patriarchs and prophets, He reminded them of His love ...

finally God became man just to enkindle in men's hearts the love of God ...

that explains—

Bethlehem and the Crib ...

Nazareth and the carpentershop ...

the three years of preaching ...

the agony and death on the Cross ...

And what will I, but that it be kindled?—

Christ has done all He could ...

the rest remains with me ...

I must kindle God's love—

    in my own soul—

        by my ordinary prayers . . .

        by frequenting the Sacraments . . .

        by at least a bit of meditation . . .

        by trying to do God's will at all times . . .

        by learning to take all that comes in life as from His hands . . .

    in the souls of others—

        by setting them a good example . . .

        by letting them see from my actions that I really love Christ . . .

        by being kind to all out of love of Christ . . .

Dear Jesus, I often tell You that I want to do what You want. And now You tell me very plainly that You want the fire of Your love kindled in my own heart and in the heart of every man, woman and child in the world. That is a big job, dear Lord, too big for me; but I promise You that I will do my share. So give me grace to love You much, and then, by word, if I can, but always by example, to teach all whom I meet to love You too. That is what I promised to do when I was confirmed.

CREATED FOR HOLINESS

For we are His workmanship, created in Christ Jesus in good works.—Eph. 2:10

For we are His workmanship—

    "I am the Lord thy God . . . . Thou shalt not have strange gods before me" *(Exod. 20:23)* . . .

    "He made us, and not we ourselves" *(Ps. 99:3)* . . .

    all that we have, all that we can ever hope to have, is from Him . . .

    He formed our bodies with all their strength and beauty and power . . .

    He gave us hands and feet, tongue and ears and eyes . . .

    He gave a glorious world in which to live . . .

He gave us all that we eat and wear and use ...

He gave us the sky with its birds, the earth with its animals, the sea with its fishes ...

He gave us the power to know and understand His creatures ..

He gave us the power to know and understand Himself ...

Created in Christ Jesus—

but above all these natural gifts, God has given us the marvelous supernatural gifts of grace ...

He has "created" us in Christ Jesus by making us one with Christ in His Mystical Body ...

and therein we are given—

sanctifying grace ...

countless actual graces ...

the seven Sacraments, each with its special grace and helps ...

Holy Mass wherein daily He renews the Sacrifice of the Cross ...

and that constant oneness with Him that is the greatest prize of life ...

In good works—

we are "created in Christ Jesus" for one only purpose: to become saints ...

do we always remember that?

do we strive constantly to become saints? ...

good works—

of thought ...

of word ...

of deed ...

good works—

for my own self ...

for others ...

good works—

at home ...

at work ...

when at play ...

when dancing ...
when with my friends ...
when alone with God ...

Dear Jesus, how good You have been to me to make me one with You in Your Mystical Body. You are holy; then I must be too. And that is precisely why You have made me one with You, isn't it? Please help me to remember that all the time; and help me, too, by Your strong graces to become really holy.

GOD'S CHANGELESS LOVE

And when He {God} passed before him, he {Moses} said: O the Lord, the Lord God, merciful and gracious, patient and of much compassion, and true.—Exod. 34:6. The Words of Moses on Mount Sinai

O the Lord, the Lord God—

eternal, unchanging and unchangeable ...

all-wise and all-powerful ...

to whom a thousand years are as a single day ...

who "reaches from end to end mightily" *(Wis. 8:1)* ...

"Maker of heaven and earth, and of all things visible and invisible" *(Creed)* ...

Merciful and gracious—

despite His greatness, or rather because of it, "merciful and gracious" ...

eager to forgive sin ...

quick to forget wrongdoing ...

anxious to bring the wandering sheep back home ...

so mindful of wayward man that He came all the way down from Heaven to save him ...

loving man so much that He has stayed with him in the tabernacle ...

Patient—

> putting up with our weaknesses . . .
> tolerant of our sloth . . .
> bearing even with our insolence . . .
> beyond all our deserving or our claims on His mercy . . .

And of much compassion—

> even in the Old Law God said to the sinful Jews: "I have remembered thee, pitying thy youth, and the love of thy espousals, when thou followedst me in the desert, in a land that is not sown" *(Jer. 2:2)* . . .
> and in the New Law He said: "Come to me, all you that labour, and are burdened, and I will refresh you" *(Matt. 11:28)* . . .

And of much compassion—

> on our bodily infirmities . . .
> on the waywardness of our minds . . .
> on the slackness of our wills . . .
> on our imperfections . . .
> on our sins . . .

And true—

> He has promised His mercy, and He will stand by His promise . . .
> He has given us His love, and He is always our Changeless Friend . . .
> He has pledged us Heaven, and, sin as we may, He still awaits us there . . .

Dear Jesus, far, far beyond any wildest dream of Moses, You are, in very truth, merciful and gracious, patient and of much compassion and true. That means so much to me in this changing, fickle world. I too am changing and fickle even in my service and love of You. That is why it is good to realize that I can always turn to You and never be refused a welcome. Just give me grace to become a little more unchanging like You.

CHEERFUL HOLINESS

Christ, our passover, has been sacrificed; therefore let us keep festival with the unleavened bread of sincerity and truth.—Communion of the Mass of Easter, Based on 1 Cor. 5:8

Christ, our passover, has been sacrificed—

> the deliverance of the Jews from Egypt had as its prelude the Paschal Lamb which was the Passover . . .
>
> and the deliverance of the whole world from the bondage of sin was preluded by the Last Supper . . .
>
> this Last Supper was itself the anticipated Sacrifice of the Cross by which we were redeemed . . .
>
> "Jesus Christ came into the world to save sinners, of whom I am the chief" *(1 Tim. 1:15)* . . .

I too can rightly call myself "chief" among sinners—

> for I know God's marvelous graces to me . . .
>
> and I know that other men have received far fewer graces than I . . .
>
> and I also know how ungrateful I have been . . .

Let us therefore keep festival—

> gloom has no lawful place in true holiness . . .
>
> God wants us to rejoice spiritually all the time . . .
>
> but the great feasts are days of special joy . . .
>
> and Easter is the cause of greatest rejoicing for by His Resurrection Christ completed our redemption . . .

With the unleavened bread of sincerity and truth—

> the Jews kept the Pasch by eating unleavened bread, an outward, material thing . . .
>
> we Christians, children of the spirit, must ourselves be the unleavened bread—
>
> > by freedom from the leaven of moral corruption . . .
> >
> > by avoidance of even the slightest sin . . .
> >
> > by an eager love of God . . .
> >
> > by the sincerity and truth of our lives . . .

then St. Paul's words will be true: "Purge out the old
leaven, that you may be a new paste, as you are
unleavened" *(1 Cor. 5:7)* . . .

Dear Jesus, help me to prepare for Easter and to celebrate it
as I should. That means that I try more and more each day
to avoid all wrongdoing and, even more than that, that I grow
daily in Your love and in my love of doing what You want me
to do. And let me do all this with joy, for it would be a sad
thing if love of You brought sadness. No other love does. Why
should Yours?

LOVE GOD SUPREMELY

**This only take care of with all diligence, that you
love the Lord your God.**—Josue 23:11

This only take care of with all diligence—

Josue in his old age leaves his parting advice to the Jews . . .
and what he said to them is far more applicable to us who
have experienced more of God's love . . .
yet there are many things we must inevitably take care of in
life—
food and clothing . . .
our work and permanence therein . . .
our loved ones and their health and security . . .
but even so there is one supreme thing of which we must
have care: "Thou shalt love the Lord thy God with thy
whole heart, and with thy whole soul, and with thy
whole strength" *(Deut. 6:5)* . . .

That you love the Lord your God—

we owe all our love to God, for—
He created us . . .
and conserves us in existence . . .
He is our Father . . .
He is our Redeemer . . .
He is our Sanctifier . . .

He pleads for our love: "Put me as a seal upon thy heart, as a seal upon thy arms; for love is strong as death" *(Cant. 8:16)* ...

and even from a selfish motive it were wise for us to love God best for: "Seek ye therefore first the kingdom of God, and His justice, and all these things shall be added unto you" *(Matt. 6:33)* ...

O my God, You know that I really want to love You above all things and all persons, even those nearest and dearest to me. I love them, yes, and You want me to love them; but it is You that I want to love best. Don't ever let me be false to Your love, no not even in little things. Let me grow in Your love every day so that my life here below may be a real beginning of an eternal life of love of You in Heaven.

GOD'S GIFT OF HIS SON

For a Child is born to us, and a Son is given to us, and the government is upon His shoulder.—Isa. 9:6.
Used as the Introit of the Third Mass on Christmas

A Child is born to us—

the Child that was promised in the Garden of Eden ...

the Child whom God foretold to Abraham as his son ...

the Child whom Jacob foresaw as bringing blessings to his house ...

the Child of whom David sang ...

the Child whom the prophets visioned ...

To us—

to all the world from Adam's day until the General Judgment ...

to the pagans of old, even in their ignorance ...

to the Jews of old, as their foreseen Messias ...

to us of the New Law, as our loved Redeemer ...

A Son is given to us—

> Eternal Son of God the Father ...
> Eternal Wisdom of the Godhead ...
> Mary's Son—
>
>> born in time ...
>> born of her alone ...
>> born in a stable ...
>> wrapped in swaddling clothes ...
>> laid in a manger ...
>> heralded by angels' song ...
>> worshiped by shepherds and Magi ...

To us—

> to each one of us, individually and separately ...
> to each one of us—
>
>> to be acknowledged by faith ...
>> to be looked forward to by hope ...
>> to be loved by charity ...
>
> to me, just as though no one else existed ...
> shall I receive the Child, and accept the Son? ...

Dear Infant Jesus, thank You, yes, thank You from my heart, for coming to me in the Crib at Bethlehem. But thank you much more for staying with me in the Tabernacle Crib of the altar. Teach me to come to You there and to love You there; and let me learn to make Your home my home.

BE A WORTHY CHILD OF GOD

For you are all the children of God by faith, in Christ Jesus.—Gal. 3:26

For you are all—

> not only those of my own family ...
> not only those of my own race and tongue ...
> not only those the color of whose skin is the same as mine ...
> but each and every man, woman and child in the whole wide world ...

The children of God—

> not aliens from Him . . .
>
> not merely creatures, the handiwork of His Omnipotence . . .
>
> but dearly beloved children . . .
>
> "Therefore you are no more strangers and foreigners; but you are fellow citizens with the saints, and members of God's household" *(Eph. 2:19)* . . .
>
> so loved by Him that He became one of us and died for each of us . . .

By faith in Christ Jesus—

> *by faith—*
>
> > grace came to us because we believed God's word . . .
> >
> > and the adoptive sonship of God came through grace . . .
> >
> > and an increased faith always means greater nearness to God . .
>
> *in Christ Jesus—*
>
> > because we have believed Him to be the Son of God . . .
> >
> > because we have placed all our hope in Him . . .
> >
> > because we are one with Him in His Mystical Body—
> >
> > > sharing His divine nature through sanctifying grace . . .
> > >
> > > having as our own the Sacrifice of the Mass . . .
> > >
> > > enriched plentifully and continually by the Sacraments . . .
> >
> > because we look forward to being with Him in Heaven unendingly . . .

Dear Jesus, how can I thank You for all Your lavish goodness to me! You gave me not only my human nature by which I am a creature, but the far greater gift of my super-nature, sanctifying grace, by which I am a child of God. Please help me to remember that always; and please help me, too, never to do anything unworthy of a child of God.

GOD IS ALWAYS KIND

Hear me, O Lord, for Thy mercy is kind; look upon me according to the multitude of Thy tender mercies.—Ps. 68:17.

(Used as the Antiphon for the Blessing of the Ashes)

Hear me, O Lord—

at the beginning of the holy season of Lent, we call upon God...

for we are His creatures and His own handiwork...

and more, we are His children, sharing in His nature through sanctifying grace...

and we are brothers of Jesus Christ, true God and true Man...

and we are members of His Mystical Body...

and so we have every reason to expect to be heard by Him...

For Thy mercy is kind—

but, when we have sinned, we have ceased to be His children and are only His creatures...

and then we rightly wonder whether He will hear us...

but He will, for His "mercy is kind"—

it was kind after the sin in Paradise...

it was kind after the sins that brought the deluge...

it was kind after the idolatry of the Jews at Mount Sinai...

it was kind after the Jews had sinned and sinned again...

it was kind after David's adultery and murder...

it was kind after we had put Him to death on the cross...

Look upon me—

for we are very frail, "man is the dream of a shadow"...

and yet we are immortal...

for we are wayward, and inconstant in our love...

and yet You love us and we really want to love You...

• 49 •

According to the multitude of Thy tender mercies—

if God metes out justice only, then we are lost . . .

but we throw ourselves on His tender mercies—

shown in His becoming Man for us . . .

shown in His lowly birth . . .

shown in His life of toil . . .

shown in His Passion and death . . .

shown in dwelling with us on our altars . . .

shown every time we were sorry for our sins . . .

shown every time He becomes our food in Holy Communion . . .

Lent, then is not a time of gloom, but a time of hope . . .

a time when the floodgates of God's mercy are opened wide . . .

and that is the constant refrain in all the Lenten liturgy . . .

Dear Jesus, I thank You from my heart that You have let me know that Your mercy is kind, and that You have shown me that Your tender mercies are manifold. I need to remember this when I have sinned, for it is then that the devil would tempt me to despair of forgiveness. And so I shall come to You always, even when I have sinned—though I sincerely hope I shall not sin— and I shall be sure of Your love. Thank You for that!

I AM CHRIST'S KEEPSAKE

For I know whom I have believed, and I am certain that He is able to keep that which I have committed unto Him against that day.—2 Tim. 1:12

For I know whom I have believed—

St. Paul had been struck down on the road to Damascus . . .

and in his blindness he recognized Christ as God and as the Messias . . .

and from that moment until his martyrdom, he never once had the slightest doubt about Christ . . .

I too have known Christ—

His mercy on me...
His patience with me...
His forgiveness of my sins...
His love for me...
and I know that He is my *Changeless* Friend...

And I am certain that He is able to keep that which I have committed unto Him against that day—

St. Paul thought of all that Christ had given him—
an immortal soul...
a miraculous call to the Church...
a vocation to be the Apostle of the Gentiles...
and he was certain that Christ would help him keep it all "against that day" by which he meant the day when Christ would come to judge him at death...

and I too should be confident that Christ will guard my trust—
the trust of my faith...
the trust of my purity...
the trust of my sanctifying grace...
the trust of my zeal for souls...
the trust of my active Catholicism...

and He will guard it if only I—
say my prayers...
come to visit Him in the Blessed Sacrament...
receive Him often in Holy Communion...
try constantly to grow in His love...
then "that day," the day of death, will have no fears for me...

Dear Jesus, how glad I am that I know You and all Your goodness and all Your love for me. That is the greatest gift of all the gifts You have given me. Thank You for it all and let my love for You and my trust in You grow every day, until the day You call me home. Keep me as Yours, and see me safe through this world until I become Your keepsake in heaven for ever.

KEEPING OUR EYES ON HOME

Therefore if you be risen with Christ, seek the things that are above, where Christ is sitting at the right hand of God.—Col 3:1

If you be risen with Christ—

> through Baptism, in which you were mystically buried with Him...
>
> through Confirmation, wherein you were strengthened by Him...
>
> through Penance, wherein your sins against Him were forgiven...
>
> through the Holy Eucharist, wherein He became your nourishment...

Seek the things that are above—

> God made many attractive things for us and we rightly yield to their attraction...
>
> but our hearts must not finally rest in them...
>
> for they are not our end...
>
> and many things here below unlawfully attract us...
>
> and to these attractions we have yielded in the past...
>
> but now, risen with the risen Christ—
>
>> our gaze must be fixed on Heaven...
>>
>> and our hearts must be always yearning for home...
>>
>> thither must our prayers ascend...
>>
>> from there we must draw the inspiration of our lives...
>>
>> and while laboring here, we must make our labor be for God...
>>
>> and while taking of earth's pleasures, we must think of the truer joys of Heaven...
>>
>> and we must prize most highly, always and everywhere, the things of eternity...

Where Christ is sitting at the right hand of God—

> "always living to make intercession for us" *(Heb. 7:25)*...

• 52 •

watching our earthly careers most interestedly ...
longing to have us come home to Him ...

Dear Jesus, You died and rose again from the dead for me. Let me die to myself and to sin and to all merely earthly desires. If I do take the good things of the world which You have made for me, let me enjoy them, as You would have me enjoy them, as foretastes of finer joys in Heaven. And, no matter where I am or with whom I may be, let me keep my eyes on home, where seated at the right hand of God You are expecting my arrival.

SEEK GOD ALWAYS

Seek ye the Lord, and be strengthened: seek His face evermore.—Ps. 104:4

Seek ye the Lord—

by knowing His wishes ...
by doing His will ...
by prayer—
in the morning and evening ...
before and after meals ...
at the Angelus ...
in visits to the Blessed Sacrament ...
in times of trial ...

Seek ye the Lord—

even though most men do not know Him ...
even though many who know Him do not seek Him ...
even though many who seek Him do so half-heartedly ...

And be strengthened—

in our memories, that we may think of God oftener ...
in our minds, to know Him better ...
in our wills—
to grow stronger against temptation ...
to live more holily daily ...

Seek His face evermore—

in youth, when the tide of life runs strong...
in mature life, when the tide of life is at its flood...
in declining years, when the tide of life is ebbing fast...

Seek His face evermore—

in days of sunshine, lest we run too greedily after pleasure...
in dark days, lest the shadows of the crosses frighten us away
from Him..
in the days of colorless routine, that we may not rebel against
life's slow grind...

Dear Jesus, I always need You, but sometimes I need You very badly. Pleasures have a way of distracting me from You, and crosses can make me grow rebellious. Even the very hum-drum of life can irk me. So give me grace to seek You always. Then I shall be strong and brave and true to You. Give me the grace to seek Your face evermore.

GOD THINKS OF ME ALWAYS

**The thoughts of His heart to all generations . . . .
to deliver their souls from death, and feed them in
famine.—**Introt of the Mass of the Sacred Heart, Taken
from Ps. 32:11,19

The thoughts of His heart to all generations—

"[God] ... reacheth from end to end mightily, and ordereth
all things sweetly" *(Wis. 8:1)*...
"Are not two sparrows sold for a farthing? and not one of
them shall fall on the ground without your Father"
(Matt. 10:29)...
God foresees everything, and He always has "my best interests
at heart"...
and so I know that nothing has happened or can happen to
me without His knowledge and consent...
and I also know that He wants everything to contribute to
my eternal salvation...

To deliver their souls from death—
> "As I live, saith the Lord God, I desire not the death of the wicked . . . . Turn ye, turn ye from your evil ways: and why will you die, O house of Israel?" *(Ezech. 33:11)* . . .
> and just precisely that I might not die the death of sin, God became Man for me . . .
> and to save me from the death of sin, He gives me—
>> the Sacrament of Holy Eucharist which nourishes me unto holiness . . .
>> the Sacrament of Penance to raise me if I am dead from sin . . .

And feed them in famine—
> the famine of the body, but much more of the soul . . .
> and there is a great soul-famine in the world today . . .
> yet we have only to turn to God and He will feed us . . .
> that is one of the great consolations of my Catholic faith that I never need be soul-hungry for a single instant . . .
> "I am the bread of life: he that cometh to me shall not hunger: and he that believeth in me shall never thirst" *(John 6:35)* . . .

Dear Jesus, it is good to know that You are always thinking about me and always deeply interested in me. That means much to me at all times but especially in my hours of darkness. Please never let me forget that, no matter how alone or how blue I may seem to be. Feed me always in my famine and deliver my soul from sin, even the slightest sin. I know You will, because You think of me always.

WE ARE GOD'S KINGDOM

Thou hast redeemed us, O Lord, in Thy blood; and hast made us a kingdom for our God.—Versicle and Response for Vespers of the Feast of the Most Precious Blood, Based on Apoc. 5:9,10

Thou hast redeemed us, O Lord, in Thy blood—
> in Adam we had all sinned and lost our supernatural destiny . . .

then we were without hope except through God's mercy...
and God was merciful and became Man to redeem us...

and He redeemed us in His blood—
> in the bloody sweat in the Garden...
> in the scourging...
> in the crowning with thorns...
> in the nailing to the Cross...
> in the thrust of Longinus' spear...

and Heaven is opened once again to us...
and sanctifying grace may be ours for the asking...
"the mercies of the Lord that we are not consumed"
> (Lam. 3:22)...

And hast made us a kingdom for our God—

throughout the Gospels Christ speaks of His kingdom...
in this world, His kingdom is His Mystical Body which is ourselves—
> to be made holier members each day...
> to be made more loyal servants of God...
> to grow more zealous to spread His kingdom...
> to become daily more avid of the riches of that kingdom...

in the next world His kingdom is Heaven—
> whither we hope to come, through His helping grace...
> where we shall be *at home* with Him for ever...
> when unalloyed happiness will be ours for all eternity...
> —if only we are worthy members of His kingdom now...

Dear Lord, after Adam sinned You could have left me in the misery to which he had reduced me. But You were good enough to come down from Heaven and to redeem me by Your Passion and death. From my heart, I thank You for Your mercy. I want to prove my gratefulness to You by being a worthy, holy member of Your Mystical Body now, so that, when You call me, I shall be one with You in Heaven for all eternity.

BE PROUD TO BE GOD'S

Every one therefore that shall confess Me before men, I will also confess him before my Father who is in Heaven.—Matt. 10:32

Every one that shall confess Me before men—

Every one—

> young or old...
> rich or poor...
> in low or high position...

That shall confess Me before men—

> by word, when there is need or opportunity...
> by deed, always—
>> doing my duties well...
>> keeping a proper self-restraint...
>> lending a helping hand...
>> thinking, speaking, acting always as a Catholic...

Every one that shall confess Me before men—

> at home...
> at school or work...
> at play...

I also will confess him before My Father who is in Heaven—

> by rewarding him with the vision of God...
> by allowing him to associate with My Mother Mary...
> by giving him the companionship of the saints and the angels...
> by giving an eternity of happiness in return for a few years of service...
> for I reward with full measure, pressed down and overflowing...
> my promise stands: "I shall be your reward exceeding great" *(Gen. 15:1)*...

Dear Lord, You know I want to love and serve You and yet I find this a bit hard at times. You have put many good things in the world for me to enjoy and I thank You very much for them. But sometimes I want to enjoy them too much; and sometimes I find it troublesome to do the right thing; and sometimes I begin to be ashamed that I am Yours. But I do want to be true to You and to acknowledge always that I am Yours. Give me grace to do this, please, because I want You to acknowledge me as Yours for ever in Heaven.

LET'S GO TO BETHLEHEM

Let us go over to Bethlehem, and let us see this word that is come to pass, which the Lord hath showed to us.—Luke 2:15

Let us go over to Bethlehem—

in memory, to the original Bethlehem—

with its narrow streets and crowded houses...

with its inn in which "there was no room" for God...

with its stable and manger which were our first gifts to Our Saviour...

by actual visit, to our Bethlehem of today—

to the Crib—

where the sheep look on inquiringly...

where Mary and Joseph kneel in adoration...

where our Infant Saviour lies with arms outstretched to win our love...

to the Tabernacle—

where our Infant Saviour is, really and truly and substantially...

where He eagerly awaits our visits...

and more eagerly longs to be united with us in Holy Communion...

And let us see this word that is come to pass—

God, a child ...
Omnipotence, weakness ...
Omniscience, helplessness ...
Offended Majesty, a pleader for our love ...

Which the Lord hath showed to us—

by the revelation of His Gospels ...
in the gift of faith which came to each of us personally in Baptism ...
by His many holy inspirations that have come to us so plentifully throughout life ...
by the special favors He will give us during the holy days of Advent and the holier days of Christmastide ...

Dear Jesus, during Advent I will try hard to prepare myself worthily for Your coming. I will do this by coming to You in Your tabernacle home where I can visit You as really as I could have done if I had been alive that first Christmas night. I shall not see You; no, but that does not matter, for I know You are really there. I will come and try to spend as much time with You as I can. Then when Christmas comes, there will be much room in my heart for You, and I know You will come and stay with me, for I want You and You want me. So give me much grace to go to Bethlehem frequently these days.

THIS IS OUR HOPE

We look for the Saviour, Our Lord Jesus Christ, who will reform the body of our lowness, made like to the body of His glory.—Phil. 3:20,21

We look for the Saviour—

because we are often "mourning and weeping in this valley of tears" ...
because the joys we do have last but a short time ...
because we are really made for God and to be with Him ...
because we are "poor, banished children of Eve" ...

and to Adam and Eve and to us their children was promised
a Saviour . . .

We look for the Saviour, Our Lord Jesus Christ—

We have Him now—
by faith . . .
by His indwelling in our souls when we are in the state of
grace . . .
by His presence on our altars . . .
by His coming within us in Holy Communion . . .
but we eagerly await His future coming—
at the hour of our death to call us *home* . . .
at the General Judgment when He shall come to judge
the living and the dead . . .
in Heaven, where we shall companion with Him for all
eternity . . .

**Who will reform the body of our lowness, made like to
the body of His glory—**

mortality will put on immortality, corruption incorruption . . .
the body—
which will be no longer a burden but lighter than thinnest
air . . .
no longer liable to pain . . .
no longer slow of motion but swift as the wings of
thought . . .
and dazzlingly bright with the splendor of the noonday
sun . . .
like unto His body which now sits at the right hand of God . . .
and all the while the soul will enjoy the undimmed vision of
God Himself . . .
—for ever, and ever, and ever . . .

And so, dear Jesus, I thank You for this hope that is laid up
in my heart. What does it matter if the road of life be dark and
rough at times! What does it matter if my body be stabbed with
pain or slowed up with infirmities. That is just for a while, and
then for all eternity my body will be changed and my soul will

enjoy the sight of You for ever. Jesus, thanks to Your grace, I don't mind what happens to me now, if only You take me home with You for ever.

RE-LIVING CHRIST'S LIFE

O God, whose only-begotten Son by His life, death and Resurrection hath purchased for us the rewards of eternal salvation; grant, we beseech Thee, that meditating on these mysteries in the most holy Rosary of the Blessed Virgin Mary, we may both imitate what they contain and obtain what they promise. Through Christ Our Lord.
—Collect of the Feast of the Most Holy Rosary

O God, whose only-begotten Son by His life, death and Resurrection hath purchased for us the rewards of eternal salvation—

Adam, our first parent, was given the promise of Heaven and the graces thereto ...

but he wilfully threw everything away for himself and for us for whom he held it all in trust ...

and we were all left hopelessly bereft of Heaven and of grace ...

but Christ came, the "second Adam," and undid the mischief of our sinful father ...

and through Christ Heaven was opened again for us ...

and through Christ we have grace and all the plentiful means of grace He has placed in His Church ...

Grant, we beseech Thee, that meditating on these mysteries in the most holy Rosary of the Blessed Virgin Mary—

the Joyful mysteries, wherein we learn to take pleasures holily ...

the Sorrowful ones, wherewith we unite our own pains with His sorrows ...

the Glorious ones, which hold out for us all the gifts that will be ours after death . . .

We may both imitate what they contain—

resignation to God's will . . .
contentment in adversity . . .
trust in God's Providence . . .
patience in suffering . . .
forgiveness of our enemies . . .
joyful expectancy of complete happiness beyond the grave . . .

And obtain what they promise—

in this life, acceptance—
    of life's vicissitudes, as though sent by God . . .
    of pain, as a means to draw nearer to Him . . .
    of death, as a summons *home* . . .
    of all life's joys and happinesses as foretastes of Heaven . . .
in the next life—
    a welcome home when we die . . .
    eternal union with Him . . .
    uninterrupted seeing Him—for ever and ever . . .

Dear Jesus, it is good to turn the pages of Your life as I dwell on each mystery of the Rosary. Teach me to relive them as I think of them, and teach me to bring out their lessons in my life. Then I shall grow daily more and more like You until the day when, at Your call, I shall come home—and You will recognize me as Your own.

DEATH MEANS GOING HOME

For in Him the hope of a blessed resurrection has shone upon us, that the very ones who are saddened by the inevitable sanction of death may be cheered by the promise of future immortality. Because for Thy faithful, O Lord, life is changed, not taken away; and when the abode of this earthly sojourn is dissolved, an eternal dwelling is prepared in Heaven.—Preface for the Mass for the Dead

For in Him—

everything we have spiritually we owe to Christ . . .

"by his bruises we are healed" *(Isa. 53:5)* . . .

He came particularly "to shine to those who sit in darkness, and in the shadow of death" *(Luke 1:79)* . . .

and surely the shadow of death lies on all of us, from the cradle to the grave . . .

The hope of a blessed resurrection has shone upon us—

Unless Christ had died for us, the grave would have held us forever . . .

"If Christ be not risen again, your faith is vain, for you are yet in your sins" *(1 Cor. 15:17)* . . .

But now as we look into the grave we realize that it is only the short, narrow tunnel that leads to life . . .

That the very ones who are saddened by the inevitable sanction of death—

"It is appointed unto men once to die" *(Heb. 9:27)* . . .

and the thought of closing our eyes on this world does sadden us and make us fear . . .

"Doth bitter death separate in this manner?" *(1 Kings 15:32)* . . .

for when death comes—

"The voice of harpers, and of musicians, and of them that play on the pipe, shall no more be heard at all in thee" *(Apoc. 18:22)* . . .

"And the light of the lamp shall shine no more in thee" *(Ibid. 23)* . . .

and even as David said to Jonathan, so can each one of us say: "There is but one step . . . between me and death" *(1 Kings 20:3)* . . .

May be cheered by the promise of future immortality—

death is coming, yes, but it is a call to come *home* . . .

and no matter how difficult the journey may be, a trip back home is always a happy one . . .

and so for us Christians, death means—

the end of toil and worry ...

the end of uncertainty ...

the reunion with our loved dead ...

the beginning of an eternity with Mother Mary and all
the saints ...

the unending companionship with God ...

death is a small price to pay for all that ...

Dear Jesus, death in itself is a dreadful thing. Even though I know the trials and sorrows of life, I know its sunshine and its joys too. Beyond the grave there would be nothing but darkness and uncertainty for me—unless You died for me. Thank You so much for dying for me for now I can await death not as a condemned man but as the summons to come *home* to you. So be it, dear Lord, so be it!

——————————

Because for Thy faithful—

for we are not "sorrowful, even as others who have no hope"
(Thess. 4:13) ...

for to us above all others Christ has said: "Where I am there
also shall my servant be" *(John 12:26)* ...

Life is changed, not taken away—

we do say as did the pagans—

"for we are born of nothing, and after this we shall be as
if we had not been" *(Wis. 2:2)* ...

"our body shall be ashes, and our spirit shall be poured
abroad as soft air, and our life shall pass away as the
trace of a cloud" *(Wis. 2:3)* ..

but we know by reason and by faith that though having had
a beginning in time, we shall live on for ever ...

Life is changed, not taken away—

our bodies go to the grave for a time, but our souls go straight
to God ...

and the things of time and of sense fall away, and we go to
   live with God for ever . . .
—if only we keep His grace here, and die in that grace . . .
then death is truly a going *home* . . .

And when the abode of this earthly sojourn is dissolved—

even as St. Paul, each of us can say: "But we had in ourselves the answer of death, that we should not trust in
   ourselves" *(2 Cor. 1:9)* . . .
for "in the sweat of thy face shalt thou eat bread till thou
   return to the earth, out of which thou wast taken: for
   dust thou art, and into dust thou shalt return"
   (Gen. 3:19) . . .

An eternal dwelling is prepared in Heaven—

"for we know, if our earthly house of this habitation be dissolved, that we have a building of God, a house not made
   with hands, eternal in Heaven" *(2 Cor. 5:1)* . . .
"as it is written: that eye hath not seen, nor ear heard, neither
   hath it entered into the heart of man, what things God
   hath prepared for them that love Him" *(1 Cor. 2:9)* . . .
truly, indeed: "O death, where is thy victory? O death, where
   is thy sting?" *(1 Cor. 15:55)* . . .
for death means to us—
   complete happiness . . .
   for ever . . .
   with God . . .

Dear Jesus, death is not a pleasant thing to dwell on if I
center all my thoughts on this life. For then it means the ending
of everything, the losing of every one and everything I love.
But, through Your own word, I know it is the beginning of all
that I could desire in my wildest dreams, and, best of all, the
beginning of being with You for all eternity. Jesus, I thank You
for having told me. I shall try to be afraid of death no longer.

FOR HIS NAME'S SAKE

O Lord, be merciful to me for Thy name's sake; because thy mercy is sweet.—Used as the Offertory for the Thursday Mass of the Third Week of Lent, based on Ps. 108:21

O Lord, be merciful to me—

    there is so much I have done, which I should not have done...
    there is so much I have not done, which I should have done...

    I need mercy, for the sins—

        of my passions...
        of my mind...
        of my memory...
        of my will...
        of my younger days...
        of my adult years...
        of the time of my ageing...

For Thy name's sake—

    I have no least claim on Your mercy...
    but You owe it to Yourself—

        for You are my Creator and You do not want Your handiwork to be spoiled...
        and all men know You are my Creator...
        for You are my Redeemer and You died for me...
        and all men know that You redeemed me...
        for You became one of us, out of love of us...
        and all men know of Bethlehem...

Your Body was tortured for me—let not that be in vain...
Your Blood was shed for me—let not that be useless...
You died a horrible death for me—let it not be fruitless...
You founded the Church for me—let it not be built to no purpose...
You instituted the seven Sacraments for me—let them not go to waste...

Because Thy mercy is sweet—
> time and time again You insist on this in the Bible . . .
> and this is the holy season of Lent "when mercy most delights
>> to spare" . . .

Because Thy mercy is sweet—
> as shown in the choosing of Your Virgin Mother . . .
> as shown in You—
>> the Babe of Bethlehem . . .
>> the Boy of Nazareth . . .
>> the village Carpenter . . .
>> the lowly "Son of Man" . . .
>> the "Man of Sorrows" . . .
>> the Victim on Calvary . . .
>> the hidden Prisoner on the altar . . .

Because Thy mercy is sweet—
> sweet when we have sinned but slightly . . .
> sweeter when we have sinned grievously . . .
> sweetest as You became our Viaticum . . .

Dear Lord, please let me always remember that wonderful phrase "for Thy name's sake." Sometimes the realization of my utter unworthiness literally terrifies me and if I dwelt much on that I would find it hard to plead with You for mercy. But I can always claim mercy and pardon and fullest forgiveness "for Thy name's sake." I wonder if You realize how much that means to me! Of course You do—for You are God—and You used it because You knew. Please help never to forget it.

OUT OF THE DEPTHS

Out of the depths I have cried to Thee, O Lord:
Lord, hear my voice.—Ps. 129:1,2

Out of the depths—
> of my sorrow, at losing a loved one . . .
> of my disappointment, in being cheated of my hopes . . .
> of my pain of body . . .

of my distress of mind...
of my chafing at the colorless routine of life...
of my joy in those I love...
of my happiness in newly-won success...

I have cried to Thee, O Lord—

at the time of morning and evening prayer...
when aspirations lifted my soul momentarily to You...
when I stopped in at the church for a "pop-call"...
when I was the living tabernacle of God after Communion...

Out of the depths, I have cried to Thee, O Lord—

with troubled spirit, yes...
but resignedly...
and trustingly...
and hopefully...

Lord, hear my voice—

for You are powerful to help me...
and You are all-wise to know the way to help me...
and You are all-merciful and so You want to help me...

Lord, hear my voice—

lest the cross weigh too heavily...
lest the pain stab too sharply...
lest the sorrow depress me overmuch...
lest the joy sweep me off my feet away from You...
lest I forget You and my home in Heaven—
where pain is no more...
where joy is full and never palls...
where You are my happiness unendingly...

Dear Jesus, in all the ups and downs of this world, I need You. Crosses weight me down and joy can take me very far from You. So I need You always, but sometimes I need You very much. So be near me at all times that I may be mindful of You and what You would have me do. Never let either joy or sorrow lessen my love for You in any way.

MAY DEEDS FULFILL FAITH

Grant, we beseech Thee, Almighty God, that for us who are bathed in the new light of Thy Incarnate Word, that which shines in our mind through faith, may be resplendent in our deeds.—Collect for the Second Mass for Christmas

Grant, we beseech Thee, Almighty God—

> all deepening of faith is a gift from God . . .
> all holier living comes from Him too . . .

For us who are bathed in the light of the Incarnate Word—

> Christ is indeed "light from light" *(Credo)* . . .
> He "inhabiteth light inaccessible" *(1 Tim. 6:16)*.
> when He came on earth a light from Heaven surrounded His choiring angels . . .
> and this sacred Christmas time, we are bathed in His light—
>> in the wonderfully joyful services of the Church . . .
>> in the graces which flood our souls . . .

That which shines in our minds through faith—

> the recognition of God's hatred of sin . . .
> the knowledge of His condescension . . .
> the conviction of His mercy . . .
> the realization of His love . . .

May be resplendent in our deeds—

> in our thoughts, so that we think as kindly of others as God does of us . . .
> in our words—
>> so that we speak of everyone as of a fellow child of God . . .
>> so that from what we say everyone may learn of God and of God's ways . . .
> in our actions, wherein we try to be as perfect as our heavenly Father is perfect . . .

so that, through us, all men may come to a better knowledge and love of God...

Dear Infant Saviour, nineteen hundred years ago You came into this world and yet after all these centuries the world does not know You. Thanks to Your great gift of faith I do know You and Your love. Give me much grace not to keep that light hidden but rather to let it shine out compellingly before all men that they may come to know and love You better. Please let Your Christmas gift to me be the grace of becoming an apostle of Your truth and love, by words, yes, but much more, and always, and everywhere, by my life itself.

EVERY DAY IS CHRISTMAS

Today you shall know that the Lord will come and save us; and in the morning you shall see His glory.—Introit of the Mass for Christmas Eve, based on Exodus 16

Today—

the first "today" was when the children of Israel murmured against God in the desert...

but since then, "today" is the "today" of each and every one of us...

for every day is "today" for God wherein He may and does show His mercy...

You shall know that the Lord will come—

to the Jews, it was by His miraculous gift of quail and manna...

to us it is His coming—

long ago, in His actual birth at Bethlehem...

now, by His manifold and multiplied graces at this holy season of Christmas...

yes, and daily and at all times by His protecting assistance and helps...

And save us—
> in the desert, it was liberation from physical death from
> starvation ..
> for us, it is liberation—
>> from all soul dangers ...
>> and from bodily dangers if it be for the good of our
>> souls ...

And in the morning you shall see His glory—
> we shall see it with our bodily eyes in the scene of Bethlehem
> unveiled once again before us ...
> we shall see it with the eyes of faith—
>> as we assist at Holy Mass ...
>> as we receive Him into the lowly manger of our bodies
>> in Holy Communion ...
>> as His grace vitalizes and invigorates our souls ...

Dear Infant God, You were very good to the starving Jews
and used Your omnipotence to help them. But you have been
far more lavish in Your goodness to me and, to speak in my poor
human way, You have taxed Your omnipotence more to do it.
You gave the Jews quails and manna; to me You have given
Yourself to be the food and nourishment of my soul. You want
every day to be a Bethlehem to me; so please give me grace to
accept Your invitation to receive You daily—eagerly, expectantly, lovingly.

THE LONELY CHRIST

**My heart hath expected reproach and misery. And
I looked for one that would grieve together with me,
but there was none: and for one that would comfort
me, and I found none.—Ps. 68:21**

My heart hath expected reproach and misery—
> from all eternity the Second Person of the Blessed Trinity
> knew that His becoming Man would mean reproach and
> misery ...

and when He became Man, He found reproach and misery—
at Bethlehem, in His birth in a stable . . .
in Egypt, as an exile . . .
at Nazareth, in poverty and as a workingman . . .
in His public life, in the opposition of the Jews . . .
in His Passion, when He was tortured and scourged . . .
in His Crucifixion, where He suffered the ultimate in
agony . . .
in His death, as the rejected outcast of His chosen
people . . .
He came to drink the cup of sorrows, and He drank it to
the dregs . . .

And I looked for one who would grieve together with
me, but there was none—
all through His life Our Lord was much alone—
the people at large misunderstood Him . . .
the Disciples and Apostles grasped but poorly who He
was and what He meant . . .
even His Blessed Mother, though she saw so deeply into
the mysteries of God, could not reach to their utmost
depths . . .
and now, how many grieve with Him—
over the sins of men? . . .
over their ingratitude? . . .
over the lukewarmness even of His friends? . . .
do I grieve with Him? . . .

And for the one that would comfort me, and I found
none—
He was in His agony—alone . . .
He was arrested—alone . . .
He was questioned—alone . . .
He was mocked and buffeted—alone . . .
He was scourged and crowned with thorns—alone . . .
He was crucified—alone . . .
what am I doing now to comfort Him—
by my own holiness? . . .

by my zeal for souls? . . .

by the example I set? . . .

by my efforts to spread His Church? . . .

Dear Jesus, You suffered much during all Your life for me and You died in terrible torments. I was not there to console You, and I wonder from my present way of living whether, if I had been there, I should have been much of a comfort to You. But I do want to be by my own life and by my efforts to bring others to You. You have been so good to me; I must try to be good to You.

HEARTS LIKE CHRIST'S

Jesus, meek and humble of heart, make my heart like unto Thine—

Jesus—

true God, from all eternity . . .

true Man, from the moment Mary said "yes" to the angel . . .

my God . . .

my Saviour . . .

Meek and humble of heart—

hiding the splendors of God to appear a Man just like myself . . .

obedient as a Child at Nazareth . . .

unassuming as the village Carpenter . . .

preaching, on foot, up and down the land . . .

a poor Man amongst poor men . . .

dying the ignominious death of the Cross . . .

Make my heart like unto Thine—

Make my heart—

filled with pride . . .

vain over the least ability I have . . .

restive under crosses . . .

chafing when thwarted . . .

easily inclined to evil . . .

quick to leave off the practice of virtue ...
readily discouraged ...
often forgetful of all Your goodness ...

Like unto Thine—

that seems an almost impossible favor ...
and only God could bring it about ...
but You *are* God ...
and You really want me to be like You ...

Dear Jesus, only You could make me like You. I am just the opposite of what You are. I am fickle, You constant; I mean, You generous; I proud, You, my God, humble; I sinful, You infinitely holy. Yet I say again: Jesus, meek and humble of heart, make my heart like unto Thine.

LIVING OUR COMMUNIONS

We entreat Thee, O Lord, that we who have been filled so completely by Thy divine Gift, may continue to live by its reception.—Postcommunion of the Mass for Saturday of Passion Week

We entreat Thee, O Lord—

we always pray to God—
humbly, because we realize our nothingness ...
reverently, because we acknowledge His greatness ...
fervently, because we know our needs ...
expectantly, because of His willing omnipotence ...

We entreat Thee, O Lord—

for ourselves ...
for our loved ones ...
for all Catholics who know Your Gift ...
for all the rest of mankind who have not yet found Your Gift ...

That we who have been filled so completely by Thy Divine Gift—

because we have assisted *integrally* at Mass by receiving Holy Communion . . .

by this "Divine Gift" which is Himself, He has completely filled us—

our bodies—

by making them His living tabernacles . . .

by being a pledge to them of a future resurrection . . .

our souls—

by His intimate real union with us . . .

by an increase of sanctifying grace in our souls . . .

by filling our minds with His ideals and principles . . .

by strengthening our wills for greater holiness . . .

May continue to live by its reception—

if Holy Communion vividly means Christ to us, then we shall receive Him frequently . . .

but frequent Communion, if not a mere formality, presupposes—

great faith, by which we actually see God in the Host . . .

great love, which makes us want to be united with Him . . .

great eagerness, which makes us count the hours until we can receive Him again . . .

"give us this day our daily bread" . . .

do I receive Holy Communion—

as frequently as possible? . . . .

as fervently as possible? . . .

do I miss Our Lord the days I fail to receive Him? . . .

Dear Jesus, there is one grace I want You to give me and that is to grow in a realization and love of You in the Holy Eucharist. You seem almost to have strained Your omnipotence to be able to be with me on the altar; and yet I show such little appreciation of You there. I am sorry for that and I now want to come and have You with me just as often as I can, and to welcome You as heartily and reverently as You deserve. You will give me this grace, won't You?

THE REWARD OF PENANCE

O God, who desirest not the death but the repentance of sinners, graciously consider the weakness of human nature and in Thy goodness deign to bless these ashes which we intend to put on our heads in token of our lowliness and to obtain forgiveness: that we, who know we are but ashes and must return to dust because of our guilt, may obtain through Thy mercy pardon of all our sins and the rewards promised to penitents. Through Christ Our Lord.—Second Prayer for the Blessing of the Ashes on Ash Wednesday

O God who desirest not the death but the repentance of sinners—

> God died for us—that is proof enough that He wants our love...
>
> and He died for us *precisely as sinners* to save us from our sins...
>
> "O Lord Our God, other lords besides Thee have had dominion over us; only in Thee let us remember Thy name" *(Isa. 26:13)*...

Graciously consider the weakness of human nature—

> "He knows the clay of which we are made"...
>
> "Compost of heaven and mire"...
>
> "One day eager and brave, the next not caring to try"...

And in Thy goodness deign to bless these ashes which we intend to put on our foreheads in token of our lowliness and to obtain forgiveness—

Lent is the time when we think long and prayerfully of our lowly conditions as men, and our lowlier conditions as sinners . . .

"pride was not made for men" *(Ecclus. 10:22)* . . .

"He hath put down the mighty from their seat, and hath exalted the humble" *(Luke 1:52)* . . .

That we who know we are but ashes and must return to dust because of our guilt—

God indeed formed man out of the slime of the earth but then gave him the gift of bodily immortality . . .

but Adam threw away the gift . . .

and then God's curse upon us all: "Dust thou art, and unto dust thou shalt return" *(Gen. 3:19)* . . .

May obtain through Thy mercy pardon of all our sins—

"Rend your hearts, and not your garments, and turn to the Lord your God" *(Joel 2:13)* . . .

"for He is gracious and merciful, patient and rich in mercy" *(ibid.)* . . .

and to us the priest has frequently said: "I absolve you from your sins, in the name of the Father and of the Son and of the Holy Ghost" . . .

And the rewards promised to the penitents—

"be of good comfort . . . For as it was your mind to go astray from God, so when you return again you shall seek Him ten times as much" *(Bar. 4:27,28)* . . .

the rewards are—

peace of soul here and sanctifying grace, too . . .

and Heaven for ever hereafter . . .

Dear Jesus, help me to enter wholeheartedly into the spirit of Lent. I have sinned against You and there is much in my life that needs correction. I will try to make amends for my sins by little acts of penance; and I will study myself so as to correct what is wrong. Just give me much grace to spend Lent well.

MARY'S GIFT OF THE KING

Adorn thy bridal chamber, Sion, and receive Christ thy King. Greet Mary, who is the Gate of Heaven; for she brings the glorious King of the new light.—Antiphon of the Procession on the Feast of the Purification

Adorn thy bridal chamber, Sion—

> we are the new Sion, the new chosen people of God...
> and we are to adorn the bridal chamber of our souls—
>> by holier thinking...
>> by a better knowledge of our faith...
>> by a clearer understanding of our duties...
>> by a more ardent love of God...
>> by a greater faithfulness in doing always what He wants of me...

And receive Christ the King—

> by an increase of sanctifying grace because of holier living...
> by more fervent participation in the Mass...
> by more loving reception of Him in Holy Communion...

Greet Mary—

> who is our constant companion for that is what her motherhood means...
> who is our guide and protector...
> who is our loving Queen...

Who is the Gate of Heaven—

> through her we have received our Redeemer who opened Heaven to us...
> she is the Mediatrix of All Graces...
> she is waiting at Heaven's gate to welcome us home...

For she brings the glorious King of the new light—

> and how we need that light in the darkened world today!...
> the light—

of God's revealed truth ...
of God's manifested love ...
of love of man for man, as redeemed children of God ...
she brings Christ to us, but we must receive Him and take
  Him from her ...
and those of us, who as her children, have already received
  Him from her must try our best to bring Him to others ...

Dear Mother Mary, you gave Our Lord to the world and you have given Him to me. And now you want to give Him to the whole world which needs Him very badly. I want to help you give Him to the world and I shall try, at all times, by thought, by word, by deed to make men know and love Him better. Help me to do this, won't you, Mother Mary?

REMEMBER WHAT GOD HAS DONE

If thou say in thy heart: These nations are more than I, how shall I be able to destroy them? Fear not, but remember what the Lord thy God did to Pharao and to all the Egyptians. — Deut. 7:17-18

If thou say in thy heart: These nations are more than
  I, how shall I be able to destroy them?—

God had saved the Jews from Pharao and his army ...
but many powerful nations blocked their way into the Promised
  Land ...
their spies had come back and told them—
  the land "hath very strong inhabitants, and the cities are
    great and walled" *(Num. 13:29)* ...
  "there we saw certain monsters of the sons of Enac
    ... in comparison of whom we seemed like locusts"
    (Ibid. 34) ...
we too get afraid and wonder—
  how we can conquer temptations ...
  how we can get over bad habits ...
  how we can be brave enough not to follow the lead of
    worthless companions ...

and in these days of the consequences of war, we all have
   much, very much to fear for ourselves and our loved
   ones . . .

**Fear not, but remember what the Lord thy God did to
   Pharao and all the Egyptians—**

if the Jews looked only to their own strength, they had every
   reason to fear . . .

but God was with them, as He had been—

   when He struck the Egyptians with the ten plagues . . .

   when He had swallowed up Pharao's army in the Red
      Sea . . .

   and He had fed the Jews with manna for forty years . . .

   and neither their clothing nor their shoes wore out during
      the forty years in the desert . . .

   surely, they should not fear if they put their trust in
      God . . .

   and I—haven't I had even more marks of God's love? . . .

   look over my life—

      Baptism, whereby I became a member of His Mystical
         Body . . .

      Confirmation, whereby I was made His soldier . . .

      Confession, wherein He forgave me again and again . . .

      Holy Communion, when He made my body His
         home . . .

   can't I, shouldn't I, trust Him to help me win the fight? . . .

   His love and protection in the past, is a pledge of His
      love and protection for all time . . .

Dear Jesus, I do find it hard at times to keep on fighting to
try to be what You want me to be. I get tired and frightened too.
But that doesn't do me any good, and it is very unfair to You.
But no matter what the odds are against me, I promise to rely
on Your grace to win the fight—and I know I cannot lose.

CHRIST'S FIRE ON THE EARTH

I am come to cast fire on the earth: and what will I, but that it be kindled?—Luke 12:49

I am come—

out from eternity into time ...
from omnipotence to helpless Infancy and Childhood ...
from possessing everything to a manger in a stable ...
from being only God to being Man too.
from eternal happiness to a death on the Cross ...
from unending life to a tomb ...

To cast fire on the earth—

My one and only purpose was to save men's souls and bring
    them back to Heaven ...
that is why I am called Jesus, "Saviour" ...

To cast fire on the earth—

the fire of love of man for God ...
the fire of love of man for his fellow men ...
the fire of zeal for the spread of My Church ...
the fire of faith that sees all things with the eyes of God ...
the fire of hope that looks forward to Heaven as home ...

And what will I, but that it be kindled?—

I have chosen all men to help me in the working of saving
    souls ...
and more especially all Catholics, for they belong to My true
    Church—
    for they pledged that at their confirmation ...
    for they are My Mother's "companions" ...
    for they know My thoughts and desires best ...

And what will I, but that it be kindled?—

never was there more need of *My* fire than today ...
today the world is filled—
    with unbelief, and a vivid faith must be brought to it
        again ...

• 81 •

with despair, and its eyes must be lifted to Heaven...

with hatred of God and man, and the fires of love must
be fanned bright and consumingly again...

My Mother's other child—what are you doing to carry out
My wishes?...

Dear Jesus, I must not disappoint You, especially now when
You need me most of all. Hardly ever have men had less knowledge of You and loved You less. And the world is filled with
distrust of man for man and hatred of each other. I do want to
do my share to enkindle in all hearts Your faith, Your hope,
Your love. I'll try to do it every day, dear Lord, by word, yes,
but much more by every action of my life. Please help me!

LETTING OUR LIGHT SHINE

**So let your light shine before men, that they may
see your good works, and glorify your Father, who
is in Heaven.—Matt. 5:16**

So let your light shine before men—

just as the lamp is placed upon the lampstand that it may
shed its rays...

so do you hold up your light to shine before men—
in the inner sanctuary of your home...
in the public walks of life...
in sickness...
in health...
in hours of joy and merrymaking...
in the days that are dark with anxieties...
in youth and in older years...

That they may see your good works—

so that they may realize that goodness has not gone out of
the world...

so that they may catch the contagion of your good ways...

so that they may be encouraged themselves to do what is right . . .

so that evil men will not be the only ones who sell their wares abroad . . .

And glorify your Father, who is in Heaven—

we "parade" our good works—

not to show off . . .

not to have a "holier-than-thou" attitude . . .

not to win favor and praise from men . . .

but we are good and we deliberately appear good—

so that God may be seen to have His followers too . . .

so that the holiness of God may be mirrored at least a bit in us for other men to see . . .

so that men may know His love, His gentleness, His mercy from our own way of acting . . .

and we do all this because we want to be "credits" to God . . .

and we want to show what Omnipotence can make out of frailty . . .

and we want to be monuments to the glory of His grace . . .

praying all the while: "not to us, O Lord, not to us; but to Thy name give glory" (Ps. 113:1) . . .

Dear Jesus, I must not "hide my light under a bushel" and fail to let men see what good things You have wrought in my life by Your grace. I must let all see what You have made out of poor, weak, sinful me. Then they too will take hope and try to lead good lives. But when I do show my good works, please do not let even the slightest bit of pride or of self sneak in. That would not be fair, for if I am any good at all, You and You alone made me what I am.

CHRIST'S THOUGHTS ABOUT US

**The thoughts of His heart to all generations . . . .
To deliver their souls from death, and feed them
in famine.**—Ps. 32:11,19. Used as the Introit of the
Mass of the Feast of the Most Sacred Heart

The thoughts of His heart—

from all eternity God determined to create mankind, and His
purposes were many and marvelous—
to give man the natural gifts of body and of soul . . .
and a goodly world to live in . . .
and much to eat and drink and much to enjoy through all
of his five senses . . .

but over and above all that, he gave man, through Adam a
high and greater gift—
sanctifying grace now, and the face-to-face vision of Himself hereafter . . .
immortality of the body, freedom from disease, perfect
self-control . . .

and even when Adam had cast all these aside God gave mankind a second chance for Heaven through the death of the
God-made-Man . . .

then when Christ had come and gone, He left His Church
to be the channel of His manifold graces . . .

To all generations—

at no single instant of time has God neglected man . . .
at no moment has He withheld grace from man . . .
from birth to the grave "the purposes of His heart" are to
bring us home to Him in Heaven . . .

To deliver their souls from death—

than ordinarily mindful that one of these days I must leave this
not from the death of the body, for that is the common penalty
of original sin . . .

but from the death of sin—

by giving grace in advance to avoid sin ...

by calling and helping to repentance after sin ...

by bestowing graces that will make us strong in virtue ...

And feed them in famine—

again, not the famine of the body, which is but a physical evil ...

but the famine of the soul—

feeding our minds with the truths of His Revelations ...

enriching our souls with the abiding presence of sanctifying grace ...

nurturing us on His own Sacred Body and Blood ...

and this after all our faithlessness to Him! ...

Dear Jesus, how can I ever thank You for Your continual thought and care of me! And it isn't as though this cost You nothing. You came down from Heaven, lived a hard life on earth and died a harder death on the Cross. And even though You had done all this for me, I have paid You back very poorly. I am truly sorry now and while I thank You for all Your thinking about me, I humbly ask Your pardon for my sins and Your grace to treat You better in the future.

BE READY ALWAYS

Watch ye, therefore, for you know not when the lord of the house cometh: at even, or at midnight, or at the cock-crowing, or in the morning, lest coming on a sudden, he find you sleeping. And what I say to you, I say to all: "Watch."—Mark 13:35-37

Watch ye therefore, for you know not when the Lord of the house cometh—

God is the master of our lives; for to Him we owe each and everything we have ...

and when He comes He will require an exact accounting—
    of every thought . . .
    of every word . . .
    of every act . . .
    of the way we used our souls and our bodies . . .
    of the way we used our mind and will and senses . . .
    of the worldly goods we have gained . . .
    of duties of our state of life . . .
it will not be the reckoning of a taskmaster . . .
but the scrutiny of a loving Father, exacting yet understanding . . .

At even, or at midnight, or at the cock-crowing, or in the morning—
    no time of life is secure from death . . .
    newborn babies die; and boys and girls; and middle-agers; and feeble oldsters . . .
    God has a right to call us home whenever He wants . . .
    and when He calls His summons must be obeyed . . .
    I know not when death will come . . .
    but I know that is nearer now than it has ever been . . .

Lest coming on a sudden, He finds you sleeping—
    forgetful of the commandments . . .
    unmindful of His love . . .
    not awake to the many opportunities for good . . .

And what I say to you, I say to all: "Watch"—
    fulfill My commandments . . .
    obey the laws of My Church . . .
    fulfill the duties of your state of life . . .
    be vigilant in prayer . . .
    be lovingly expectant of My coming . . .

Dear Jesus, during the holy season of Lent, let me be more than ordinarily mindful that one of these days I must leave this world and come home to You. There are many things here to make me forget You and the life beyond the grave. But I must not forget. So I will try hard at all times, but especially during this holy season of penance, so to live that whether You come in the evening, or at midnight, or at cock-crow, or early in the morning, You will find me ready to come home at once to You.

SIMEON ONCE, I ALWAYS

Now Thou dost dismiss Thy servant, O Lord, according to Thy word in peace; because my eyes have seen Thy salvation, which Thou hast prepared before the face of all peoples: a light of revelation to the Gentiles, and the glory of Thy people Israel.—Luke 2:29-32. Part of the Gospel of the Feast of the Purification

Now Thou dost dismiss Thy servant, O Lord, according to Thy word in peace—

Simeon had been told by "the Holy Ghost that he should not see death before he had seen the Christ of the Lord" *(Luke 2:26)* ...

and he had lived his life amid the turmoil of Jerusalem in calmest expectation ...

and now having seen Christ and held Him in his arms, life ceases to attract him any longer ...

and he looks for death as its peaceful close ...

and so with me who know God well—

my life should be one of inner calm despite the trials of life ...

and my eyes should be fixed on the mysteries of faith in this life, and on Heaven, their fulfillment in the next ...

and death should hold no terrors for me but just be the way of going home to God in peace ...

Because my eyes have seen Thy salvation, which Thou hast prepared before the face of all peoples—

Simeon, after years of waiting, had at length gazed on the "Christ," the anointed Saviour of mankind ...

and he knew that the thousands of years of waiting had
brought their promise . . .

I too have seen God's "salvation" and in a greater way—
the entire life of Christ, closed with the final act of
redemption . . .

the Church, which is His Mystical Body, extended through
time and space . . .

Himself in the Holy Eucharist, where He is our con-
tinuing salvation . . .

A light of revelation to the Gentiles—

because He was come "to shine on those who sit in darkness,
and in the shadow of death" *(Luke 1:79)* . . .

from the pagan Gentiles the fuller light of God's revelation
had been kept hid by reason of their own sinfulness . . .

but after Christ's coming, the voice of God's ministers "hath
gone forth into all the earth, and their words unto the
ends of the world" *(Ps. 18:5)* . . .

truly "they have sought me that before asked not for me. I
said: 'Behold me, behold me,' to a nation that did not call
upon my name" *(Isa. 65:1)* . . .

The glory of thy people Israel—

Christ was indeed the crowning glory of Israel, for toward
Him its whole two thousand years of history had been
molded . . .

"God, who, at sundry times and in divers manners spoke in
times past to the fathers by the prophets, last of all, in
these days hath spoken to us by His Son" *(Heb. 1:1,2)* . . .

yet at Pilate's Judgment Seat Israel officially rejected its
Glory . . .

and now we are the new Israel, and we should make Christ
be our glory—

enshrining Him in our hearts as our true King and the
master of our lives . . .

receiving Him often in Holy Communion and thus
becoming His living tabernacles . . .

honoring Him by our external conduct . . .

making Him known and loved by the manner of our lives . . .

Dear Jesus, Simeon was very happy to see You once and to hold You once in his arms. For this he had waited many, many years, and waited most willingly. What Simeon had once, I have always through Your gracious kindness. But I do not appreciate You the way I should. I must change this, and I must make You the glory of my life, inside my soul, and in my dealings with others. So give me grace, much grace to appreciate You as I should, and by making You my "glory" carry the light of Your revelation to each and every one I meet.

CORRECTIVE SELF-DENIAL

Grant, we plead with Thee, Almighty God, that the dignity of human nature, now wounded by self-indulgence, may be restored by the practice of corrective self-denial.—Collect of the Mass for Thursday of Passion Week

Grant, we plead with Thee, Almighty God—

when we rely on our strength, we find it only weakness . . .
and if we lean on others, their help proves very limited . . .
only from God can help come . . .
and all the help we need will come because He is almighty and all-merciful . . .

That the dignity of human nature—

if we center our minds too much on our lower nature, we can hardly find much that is worth while in us . . .
but there is a dignity in our human nature—

because man "was made to the image and likeness of God" . . .

because of our immortal soul . . .

because of our eternal destiny . . .

Now wounded by self-indulgence—

> pampering ourselves makes us over-grown "spoiled children" . . .
> and self-indulgence wounds our dignity—
>> because it lets our lower desires and passions gain control . . .
>> because it darkens our minds and weakens our wills . . .
>> because it makes us less worthy of God's graces . . .

May be restored by the practice of corrective self-denial—

> if a tree is bent, it must be bent in the opposite direction to bring it to be straight . . .
> and self-denial does this—
>> because it brings self-control . . .
>> because it makes reparation to God for sins committed . . .
>> because it enables us to be like Christ in His sufferings . . .
> since each one has sinned, each one needs this corrective self-denial . . .
> thus Holy Mother Church wisely decrees a season of penance that all her children may be restored to their proper dignity . . .
> am I restoring mine? . . .

Dear Jesus, I don't like penance and mortification. Nobody does. But You Yourself have taught me, by word and by example, that it is necessary. I have acted unworthily of my human nature, have lowered its dignity and have offended You. So I need much corrective self-denial. Help me to be brave enough to do penance and to make amends.

ALONE AND POOR

My eyes are ever towards the Lord: for He shall pluck my feet out of the snare. Look Thou upon me, and have mercy on me; for I am alone and poor.—Ps. 24:15-16. Used as the Introit of the Mass for the Third Sunday in Lent

My eyes are ever towards the Lord—

as we go through life we increasingly realize our helplessness . . .

and we realize too with startling clearness how powerless men are to aid us in any real crisis . .

and so life teaches us, if we think at all, to turn more and more to God, whose power is limitless . . .

"to Thee have I lifted up my eyes, who dwellest in Heaven. Behold as the eyes of servants are on the hands of their masters, as the eyes of the handmaid are on the hands of her mistress, so are our eyes unto the Lord our God, until He have mercy on us" *(Ps. 122:1-2)* . . .

For He shall pluck my feet out of the snare—

daily we pray: "Lead us not into temptation, but deliver us from evil" . . .

daily the priest prays in the Canon: "Deliver us, we beseech Thee, O Lord, from all evils, past, present, and to come" . . .

and God is all-powerful and all-willing to help us . . .

Look Thou upon me, and have mercy on me—

He will, for He Himself has said: "Let the wicked forsake his way . . . and let him return to the Lord . . . for He is bountiful to forgive" *(Isa. 55:7)* . . .

Again, when He walked the earth as Man, He cried out: "Come to Me, all you who labour, and are burdened, and I will refresh you" *(Matt. 11:28)* . . .

and He died on the Cross with His arms outstretched to assure us of a welcome always . . .

For I am alone and poor—

the first and essential requisite for gaining God's mercy is humility, which means lowly-mindedness . . .

"He hath scattered the proud in the conceit of their heart . . . and hath exalted the humble" *(Luke 1:51-52)* . . .

"alone and poor" we all are in the inmost recesses of our souls and in the deepest trials of life . . .

Dear Lord, in all humility I turn to You and ask Your help. Sometimes, I know, I am foolish enough to be vain and proud, and to think myself somebody. But You will forgive these silly thoughts, won't you? And You will be merciful to me, I know, and will deliver me from evil and help to bear my crosses, because —remember—You are "bountiful to forgive."

GOD IS MY STRENGTH

I love Thee, O Lord, my strength: the Lord is my firmament, my refuge, and my deliverer.

—Ps. 17:2-3. Used as the Introit for Septuagesima.

I love Thee—
> yes, I fear God—
>> because He has the power to punish me ...
>> because He has the right to send me to hell ...
>> because He is to be my Judge, from whose sentence there will be no appeal ...
>> but my fear is the reverential fear of a dutiful child, not the cringing fear of a slave ...
> and above all I love God—
>> for He is my Creator who drew me out of nothingness ...
>> for He is my Father who sent His only-begotten Son to redeem me after I had spurned His love ...
>> for He is my Redeemer who died to free me from sins ...
>> for He is my Sanctifier who dwells in my soul as in His temple ...
>> for it is from Him that I have received every single gift that I possess ...

My strength—
> I am frail physically, but God is omnipotent ...
> I am weak morally, but He is infinitely holy ...
> I am inconstant, but He never changes ...
> Left to myself I totter and fall, but I can lean on Him fearlessly ...

God is my firmament, my refuge—

to Him I can flee and be perfectly secure...
when His omnipotence shields me no one can harm me...
and He is always most willing to grant me refuge...

And my deliverer—

there is no harm from which He can not protect me...
there is no evil from which He can not free me, even when it
has come upon me...

And my deliverer—

from physical harm...
from mental anxieties...
from sin and all its consequences...
—if only I really want to be delivered...

O my God, how thoughtful Holy Mother Church is to remind me on the very threshold of Lent of Your willingness to help and protect, and, if need be, deliver me. My sinfulness terrifies me at times and at other times discourages me; and the disappointments and trials and sufferings of life almost crush me. But not if I remember Your strength, not if I recall Your love. So give me this grace, I beg of You, to be always mindful of Your power and always conscious of Your love for me; and much grace too to run to You trustingly when I need you most and yet perhaps fear to come.

HE WILL REFRESH US

**Come to Me all you that labour, and are burdened,
and I will refresh you.**—Matt. 11:28

Come—

Christ does not command, He invites...
a welcome awaits me such as I have never known before...
yet I am free to refuse...

To Me—

God infinite in power and most anxious to help...

"the Father of mercies and God of all comfort" *(II Cor. 1:33)* . . .

the gentle Man of Sorrows . . .

who loves us so much that He died for us . . .

All you that labour—

and all do labour since all are under Adam's curse: "In the sweat of thy face shalt thou eat bread till thou return to the earth, out of which thou wast taken" *(Gen. 3:19)* . . .

all that labour—

in the slow drudgery of the home . . .

in the colorless routine of the office . . .

in the rough shuffling of the business world . . .

And are burdened—

with the ordinary cares of life . . .

with illness of self or loved one . . .

with the death of one near and dear . . .

with worries about money and the necessities of life . . .

And I will refresh you—

giving us that peace which the world can not give and can not take away . . .

strengthening our wills to bear our crosses more easily . . .

lifting our hearts to Heaven and all its unending joys . . .

coming in person in Holy Communion wherein "the mind is filled with joy and there is given to us a pledge of eternal glory" . . .

Dear Jesus, I do find the road of life hard, and at times very hard. Not only must I contend against outside difficulties and trials but my own unruly self gives me a lot of trouble. So I come to You with all my burdens to have You ease them or at least make me stronger to bear them. Give me that abiding peace which is Your peace and which no one can take away.

AID FOR HIS REDEEMED

Therefore we beseech You to come to the aid of Your servants whom You redeemed by Your Precious Blood.—Verse from the Te Deum

We beseech You—

we cannot demand Your aid because we are mere creatures . . .
we dare not demand it, if we could, because of our sins . . .
and so we beseech You—

in all humility . . .
with all love . . .
with all insistency, too, as You told us to pray incessantly . . .

To come to the aid—

we are weak, and the road of life is long and rough . . .
we are fearful, and many dangers surround us . . .
we are prone to sin, and evil is very enticing at times . . .

Of Your Servants—

we are His creatures and the work of His hands . . .
and by His gracious gift His friends: "I will not now call you servants . . . but I have called you friends" (John 15:15) . .
but even more than that, we are His children: "Behold what manner of charity the Father hath bestowed upon us, that we should be called, and should be the sons of God" (I John 3:1) . . .

Whom You have redeemed—

God had given us all a chance for Heaven, but Adam threw it away . . .
and if God had left us, life should have been quite hopeless . . .
but the Second Person determined to take upon Himself our sinful nature that through it He might redeem us . . .
and when the centuries had been counted off He became Man for us . . .

By Your Precious Blood—

not merely by becoming Man . . .
not merely by suffering want and poverty . . .
not merely by working as a laboring man . . .
but by shedding His Precious Blood—

at the Circumcision . . .
in the Agony . . .
on the Cross . . .
at the Scourging . . .
when He was crowned with thorns . . .
when He walked the first Way of the Cross . . .
when He was nailed to the Cross . . .
when His Heart was pierced by the lance . . .
truly we "are bought with a great price" *(I Cor. 6:20)* . . .

Dear Jesus, You were wonderfully good and merciful to
redeem me and that too at such a price. You have given me
another chance for Heaven; but I am not there yet. So come to
my aid today, tomorrow and every morrow, for if I fail to come
home to Heaven then Your Precious Blood will have been shed
in vain. And You don't want that, do You?

OUR MOTHER'S PRAYER

**May the prayer of the Mother of God bring aid to
Thy people, O Lord; for although we know that
she has passed on as all flesh must, may we realize
that she pleads for us with Thee in the glory of
Heaven.**—Secret of the Mass for the Assumption

**May the prayer of the Mother of God bring aid to Thy
people, O Lord—**

Mray's prayer in life was powerful—
gaining for herself the motherhood of God . . .
bringing sanctification to Elizabeth and the unborn
Baptist . . .
winning for Joseph the solution of his doubt . . .

securing the first miracle at the wedding feast of Cana...
steadying the Apostles in the Cenacle after Calvary...
mothering the infant Church while she was still on
earth...
and now in Heaven—
her love for us is greater...
and her intercession with God more powerful...

For although we know that she has passed on as all flesh must—

though spared from many of the effects of original sin, she
was not spared death...
in this she was like us all, and like even her divine Son...
her death is piously believed to have been due to the excess
of her love of God..

May we realize that she pleads for us with Thee in the glory of Heaven—

she is safe, but she does not forget her children who must yet
come home...
and like her Son, she "lives always to make intercession" for
us...
and we ask God that we may realize her intercession—
by a greater love for Him and her...
by a closer imitation of Him and her...
by a fervor of life more closely resembling hers...
by a more careful attention to our least duties, such as
she showed...
by a marked help at death so that we may come to
Heaven, with her...

Dear Jesus, You have given me Your own Mother as my
Mother. You need not have done so but You did, and it was
wonderfully good of You. I need our Mother's help very much
now to lead the life You want me to lead so as to come and be
eternally home with You. So may I have her help "now and at
the hour of my death."

HIS DEPARTED SERVANTS

O God, the Creator and Redeemer of all the faithful, grant to the souls of Your departed servants and handmaids the remission of all their sins, that through fervent supplications they may obtain the pardon they have always desired.—Collect in the Mass for the Dead

O God, the Creator and Redeemer of all the faithful—

from all eternity He had determined to create us ...

and when the time, which He had set, had come, He brought us into being ...

and He gave us a wonderful supernatural destiny, which Adam threw away ...

then the Second Person mercifully determined to become Man ...

and He lived and worked and died to win Heaven back for us ...

Grant to the souls of Your departed servants and handmaids—

in life and in death they are stamped as Yours by the sacred characters of Baptism and Confirmation ...

they tried to serve You, though maybe not as well as they might ...

"for although he has sinned, he did not deny the Father, and the Son, and the Holy Ghost, but believed in them" *(Prayers for the Dying)* ...

That through fervent supplications—

the Holy Souls cannot help themselves, for their days of meriting are over ...

so, we the living, must help them—

by our prayers ...

by our good works ...

by acts of self-denial ...

by having Mass offered for them...
am I doing all I can to bring them into God's presence?...

They may obtain the pardon they have always desired—
time and again they confessed their sins to gain pardon...
daily they prayed—

> "pray for us sinners, now and at the hour of our death"...

> "forgive us our trespasses as we forgive those who trespass against us"...

> "I confess . . . because I have sinned exceedingly in thought, word and deed"...

> "may the almighty and merciful God grant me pardon, absolution and remission of all my sins"...

O my merciful Jesus, help me to bring home to You the Holy Souls who are still kept away from You. You want them home; and they want to go home to You. So I shall keep them in my prayers and shall offer up good works for them. That should be my part in the Communion of Saints. Then when they are with You I hope they will pray for me.

OUR MOST GRACIOUS LORD

Thou wast born before time from the Father without a mother, and today became Man out of Thee without a father; wherefore the star greets the Magi, the angels with the shepherds sing Thy wonderful Nativity, O most gracious One.
—From the Liturgy of the Greek Rite for
the Second Day of Christmas

Thou wast born before time from the Father without a mother—
from all eternity the Second Person proceeded from the Father alone...
"God from God, Light from Light, true God from true God"...

equal in all things with the Father, yet His Son...

that is the mystery of the Blessed Trinity which we reverently and lovingly accept...

And today became Man out of Thee without a father—

"Behold a Virgin shall conceive, and bear a Son" *(Isa. 7:14)* ...

and Mary, the humble maid of Nazareth, was the Virgin-Mother...

Joseph was her protector, and the foster father of the Man-God...

this is the mystery of the Virgin birth which we reverently and lovingly accept...

Wherefore the star greets the Magi—

calling them to worship at the manger...

calling them to adore a newborn Child...

calling them to recognize "Omnipotence in bonds"...

The angels with the shepherds sing Thy wonderful Nativity—

Bethlehem had no room for Him, but Heaven burst open with joy...

and the shepherds hastened to the stable...

"the shepherds returned, glorifying and praising God, for all the things they had heard and seen" *(Luke 2:20)* ...

O most gracious One—

no one has been more gracious to me than the Infant Saviour...

no one has been so considerate of me...

no one has gone to such lengths to win my love...

have I made return of love?...

do I now love Him as I should?...

will I, from now on, try to love Him as He deserves?...

O most gracious Jesus, You have gone to greatest lengths to win my love. You came down from Heaven, were born in a stable, lived a workingman's life, and died a cruel death—all to have me love You. I have loved You some, but not as I should. You deserve all my love and I want to give it all to You. Take it, and keep it, please—for ever.

I OWE HIM ALL

God, who, at sundry times and in divers manners, spoke in times past to the fathers by the prophets, last of all, in these days hath spoken to us by His Son.—Heb. 1:1. Used as the Little Chapter of Second Vespers of Christmas.

God, who, at sundry times and in divers manners—

in the Garden to Adam and Eve...

on the top of the raging flood to Noe...

on the mountain height as He stopped Abraham about to sacrifice Isaac...

at the stone pillow on which Jacob slept...

amid the thunder and lightning of Sinai to Moses during forty days...

to David as he sang to Israel of the future Saviour...

to Isaias as he peered deep into the future and saw the Virgin birth...

Spoke in times past to the fathers by the prophets—

at no time did God leave man without hope of a coming Redeemer...

even just after the Fall, when still recently offended, He fromised the future Christ...

and it was for that Messias that He chose Abraham and his seed...

and it was for that Messias that all the history of the Jews was shaped...

and it was around that Messias that all the hopes of the chosen people were centered...

for one day there would come—

"the Desired of all Nations"...

"the Star of Jacob"...
"the Desire of the Eternal hills"...
Emmanuel, God-with-us...

that was the 2,000 years Advent of the Jews...

but when that Advent had its Christmas, they did not know it...

when this Advent is over, will there be a true spiritual Christmas for me?...

Last of all, in these days hath spoken to us by His Son—

for "a Child is born unto us, and a Son is given to us" (Isa. 9:6)...

and He speaks to us at Bethlehem—
    from within the stable...
    lying in a manger...
    wrapped in swaddling clothes...
    nestled in His Mother's arms...

and every day He speaks to us—
    by the whisperings of His holy inspirations...
    by the holy desires of our wills...
    by the graces of the Sacraments...
    by the daily Masses offered everywhere...

we are His privileged children—
    for we know the Man-God truly born of Mary...
    we are members of His Mystical Body...
    we receive Him within us in Holy Communion...
    we may visit Him whenever we like in His altar home...

Dear Jesus, I am so happy that You came into this world before I did. If I had lived before Your time, none of the holy things that I have known from childhood would have been mine: Christmas, Good Friday, Easter, the Church, the Sacraments, Your example, Your Mother's loving care of me. That is why I am so happy at Christmas time for it brings back to me the realization of all I owe to You. Dear Jesus, in Your crib, I thank You for Your coming and all that it means and has meant to me.

CAN I RESIST HIS LOVE?

By the mystery of the Incarnate Word, a new ray of Thy glory has flashed upon the eyes of our mind, so that while we recognize God in visible form, by Him may we be swept aloft to a love of things invisible.—Preface for Christmastide

By the Mystery of the Incarnate Word—

God the unseeable is seen...
God the untouchable is touched...
God reaching everywhere is held by a manger...
God omnipotent is a helpless Babe...

A new ray of Thy glory has flashed upon the eyes of our mind—

God "inhabiteth light inaccessible" *(I Tim. 6:16)*...
but from the inner fires of the Godhead, flashes came—
when the rainbow sealed the covenant with Noe...
when lightnings brightened Sinai's summit...
when the cloud by day and the pillar of fire by night led the wandering Jews..
when the Cloud-Presence rested always over the Holy of Holies.
but now He has come among us who is—
"the image of the invisible God" *(Col. 1:15)*...
"the brightness of His glory" *(Heb. 1:3)*...
"the brightness of eternal light, and the unspotted mirror of God's majesty, and the image of His goodness" *(Wis. 7:26)*...

So that while we recognize God in visible form, by Him may we be swept aloft to a love of things invisible—

God came from Heaven to bring us to Heaven...
and His coming was due—
to His love...

to His mercy...
to His desire to have us with Him for ever...
and He came—
  in the most endearing form, that of a Child...
  in the most usual form, that of a workingman...
  in the most consoling form, that of the Man of
    Sorrows...
all, just to win my love...
have I given Him my love?...
will I give it to Him—
  unreservedly?...
  unrecalledly?...

Dear Jesus, how can anyone resist Your love! From out the crib You plead for it, a most lovable Babe, yet God. Does anyone refuse to love You? Unfortunately yes—and I among them. O! I love You a bit, but only a bit, or else I'd be a saint right now. So please give me the Christmas gift of loving You more and more; then I can give You the only gift You want—my heart.

HE NEVER FORSAKES US

Do manfully and be of good heart: fear not, nor be ye dismayed at their sight; for the Lord Thy God He Himself is thy leader, and will not leave thee nor forsake thee.—Deut. 31:6

Do manfully and be of good heart: fear not, nor be dismayed at their sight—

  we all get frightened at times at the difficulties that confront
    us...
  and we get discouraged at the slight success we seem to
    have...
  and we chafe at the monotony of a routine existence...
  "just what is the use of trying?"...
  "we can't win anyhow!"...
  —no, not if we have only our own strength to rely on...

For the Lord Thy God He Himself is thy leader—

> our hope and trust lie in God, who is all powerful ...
> the world may be all awry, but He is still watching over us ...
> man may be cruel, but He is still our loving Father ...
> men may plot our ruin, but He is our Protector ...
> this may be our hour of darkness, but He will be the Light
> of our lives ..
> "if God be for us, who is against us?" *(Rom. 8:31)* ...

And will not leave thee nor forsake thee—

> I may change, but He is my Changless Friend ...
> I may falter, but He is almighty and supports me always ...
> "the bruised reed He shall not break, and smoking flax He
> shall not quench" *(Isa. 42:3)* ...
> for "even to your old age I am the same, and to your grey
> hairs I will carry you: I have made you, and I will bear:
> I will carry and will save" *(Isa. 46:4)* ...

Dear Jesus, I do get very discouraged at times in the constant struggle of life. You know I don't want to be a quitter but I am sorely tempted at times to be done with it all. The only thing that holds me up is the consciousness that I can rely on You and Your grace and that You will never fail me even in my darkest, heaviest hour. Dear Lord, I thank You for Your unfailing help. Never let me forget that You are always at my side. That will keep me fighting until the battle of life is over and I am safe with You in Heaven.

LET CHRIST GUARD US

And the peace of God, which surpasseth all understanding, keep your hearts and minds in Christ Jesus.—Phil. 4:17

And the peace of God, which surpasseth all understanding—

> that peace which the world cannot give and cannot take
> away ...

for it comes from God and unites with God...

it is a reflection of the eternal peace that reigns between the Father, the Son, and the Holy Ghost...

it is a foretaste of the peace that will be between and in the Blessed for ever...

Keep your hearts and minds—

we need increasing vigilance—

against the devil, "who roams through the world, seeking the destruction of souls"...

against the sinful attractions that surround us...

against our own weak, fickle selves...

but we need more than our vigilance, than our strength, as our sin-filled past proves...

and so we ask God to stand guard...

then all will be safe for, "Behold he shall neither slumber nor sleep, that keepeth Israel" *(Ps. 120:4)*...

Keep your hearts and minds—

so that we may know what is right...

so that we may love what is right...

so that we may do what is right...

so that the one thing we always are most concerned about is the salvation of our soul...

In Christ Jesus—

in and through our love of Christ...

in and through our union with Him in Holy Communion...

in and through our union with Him in His Mystical Body...

Dear Jesus, stand guard over my foolish mind and wayward heart lest my soul be stolen from You or I myself wander far from You. Let Your peace be always in my heart keeping my mind close to You and my will in love with You. I can be and am "caught off guard" at times; but not You. So I put my eternal safety in Your hands—it is safe there.

WHY FEAR DEATH?

Death is swallowed up in victory. O death, where is thy victory O death, where is thy sting?
—I Cor. 15:54,55

Death is swallowed up in victory—

> to the pagan death meant at best a shadowy, ghostlike existence . . .
>
> even the Jews seemed often to have a very poor idea of life after death . . .
>
> but when Christ died, death was shown to be what it really is, the entrance into eternal happiness . . .
>
> by His death—
>
>> He rewon for us a chance for Heaven . . .
>>
>> He opened the shut doors of Heaven and ushered souls in for the first time . . .
>>
>> He merited graces for us to lead a holy life and to die a happy death . . .

O death, where is thy victory?—

> certainly not in freeing us from the cares of life . . .
>
> certainly not in taking away its fleeting pleasures . . .
>
> certainly not in taking us from exile into our Father's home . . .
>
> hardly in ushering us from the shadows of the vale of tears into the glory of eternity . . .

O death, where is thy sting?—

> in the sharp stab of pain which soon passes? . . .
>
> in the heat of fever which is quickly allayed by death's cold hand? . . .
>
> in the heavy drowsiness which will be changed to an eternity of joyous activity? . . .
>
> in the farewells to loved ones whom we shall soon meet again never to be separated? . . .

O death, where is thy sting?—
> yet the sting will be there—
>> unless we keep our souls free from sin...
>> unless we lead a life of faith...
>> unless we have much love for God...

Dear Jesus, I thank You for conquering death and all its fears too. Naturally death is a fearsome thing, and only the thought of Heaven and of Your being there to greet me makes those fears grow less. The only thing that can make death dreadful is sin; and so I beg of You to keep me always far from sin by making me grow daily in Your love.

AS THE YEARS COME AND GO

For we this day dedicate unto Him the living God by the gifts we offer, the close of the past year, and the commencement of that which follows. For by Him we have lived through the years gone by, and are about to commence the beginning of another.—Preface of the Mass before Epiphany in the Mosarabic Rite

For we this day dedicate unto Him the living God by the gifts we offer—
> by the greatest of all gifts, the Mass...
> by the gifts of our reception of Him at the altar...
> by the gift of the submission of our minds to the truths of faith...
> by the gift of the ready obedience of our wills to His law...

The close of the past year and the commencement of that which follows—
> the old year is gone for weal or for woe...
> the new year, stretches unseen and unseeable before us...
> God and I know the past; only God knows the future...
> I leave both to Him and His infinite Wisdom...

For by Him we have lived through the years gone by—

through our childhood and all its helplessness...
through our youth and its many frivolities...
through our maturer years when life's burdens began to irk...
through days of health and days of pain...
through days of joy and days of sorrow...
through days of success and days of failure...
and every day was a day of a "year of Our Lord"...

And are about to commence the beginning of another—

we stand at its beginning; but our end may come before its
end...
but God's plan will be unfolded if only we do our part...
so at its beginning we say from our hearts: "Be it done to me
according to Thy word"...
each year that passes means one less away from Father's
home.

O my God, I thank You for all the years that are gone and all the graces and blessings they brought. There was joy and there was sorrow, but always You were there too. I am grateful to You for all and I now give You myself whole and entire. I do not know what the new year will bring me. You do. I accept it from Your hands. May its end, or my end before its end, find me nearer and dearer to You!

LONG LIVE THE KING!

Jesus Christ, the King of Kings: Come, let us adore.—Invitatory from the Office of the Feast of Christ the King

Jesus Christ, King—

in the *minds* of men—

because He is truth itself, and our minds must find
truth...
because of the truths He has revealed, thus giving our
minds knowledge which would have been beyond our
reach...

because our minds subject themselves to Him by the act of faith...

because we recognize Him to be both God and perfect Man...

in the *wills* of men—

because He is the supreme Model to which we must become likened...

because our will is ennobled by its obedience to Him...

because by yielding to His grace, our will is lifted to a supernatural level...

in the *hearts* of men—

because He draws us by the bonds of His kindness and gentleness...

because no man has ever been loved as He has...

because to know Him is to love Him...

Jesus Christ, King of Kings—

because to Him has been given "all power in Heaven and on earth" by reason of the Incarnation...

because He is the Lawmaker of the New Testament...

because He is "the Judge of the living and of the dead"...

and we have entered into His earthly kingdom through faith and Baptism...

and we shall enter into His eternal kingdom if we die with His love in our hearts...

Come, let us adore—

He deserves the best we have, and our best is paltry enough...

love prompts us to do our best and give Him our best...

to adore Him now is to begin on earth what we shall spend our eternity doing in Heaven...

have I yet begun my Heaven on earth?...

Dear Lord Jesus, You have every right to be my King and I want You to be. But so far I haven't let You, at least not entirely. But I do want You to rule and govern me and everything I have. I want You to be my King in soul and in body, in my senses, my mind, my will and my heart. Let me learn to let you rule there completely—then I shall be really happy.

CAN WE FIND ONE LIKE HIM?

O all ye that pass by the way, attend, and see if there be any sorrow like to my sorrow.—Lam. 1:12

O all ye that pass by the way—
older folk who have passed along most of the way ...
mature folk who have gone quite half of the journey ...
young folk who are still at the journey's start ...
for we all pass this way only once ...
and the years that are gone are gone for ever ...
sometimes the way is smooth and sunny ...
sometimes it is dark and more than rough ...
but at the end is *home,* if only we travel aright ...
and we shall travel aright, if we look to Christ ...

Attend, and see—
the Sacred Heart of Jesus begs us to look and think ...
for "with desolation is all the land made desolate; because
there is none that considereth in the heart" *(Jer. 12:11)* ...
and we should look upon the Man of Sorrows ...
and we should come to know His sorrows ...
and we should come to realize—
that we caused them ...
and that they are all for us ...

If there be any sorrow like to my sorrow—
"behold the Man" *(John 19:5)* ...
behold Him—
in the manger—was any child poorer than He? ...
on the road to Egypt—was any child persecuted as He? ...
in the thirty hidden years—was any man as obscure as He? ...
in His public life—was anyone so misunderstood? ...
when Judas kissed Him—was anyone so betrayed? ...

• 111 •

when Herod made a fool of Him—was any man so reviled? . . .

in the three hours on the Cross—did ever human body suffer so? . . .

in the way His love has been spurned—have men ever been so ungrateful to another? . . .

and I have caused Him sorrow . . .

and maybe I am paining Him now . . .

—can I have the heart to keep on paining Him? . . .

—or shall I give Him all He asks? . . .

Dear Jesus, Man of Sorrows, let me learn to keep my gaze fixed on You. You deserve that because You suffered everything for me just as though no one else existed. And I need to keep thinking of all Your sufferings so that I may realize how terrible sin is when it could cause You to suffer so much. Yes, dear Lord, with Your grace I will think of You, the Man of Sorrows, always and everywhere until I finally come home to You.

TRUE FEAR OF GOD

Come, children, hearken unto me: I will teach you the fear of the Lord.—Ps. 33:12. Used as the Gradual in the Mass of the Fourth Sunday of Lent

Come—

God's invitation *always* stands: "Come" . . .

no matter how seriously we may have sinned, or how frequently, or how long, He still says, "Come" . . .

it is only by an impenitent death that we force Him to stop urging us: "Come" . . .

Children—

God is Our Father and we must never forget that . . .

and He does His best to have us not forget it by repeatedly calling us His children . . .

yet so many, even Catholics, look on Him as a harsh task-master and even a cruel tyrant ...

Hearken unto me—

children must always listen to learn ...
and so we, "children of a larger growth," must listen too ...
we have much to learn ...
and, unfortunately, much to unlearn ...

I will teach you the fear of the Lord—

not the cringing fear of slave of a master ...
but the respectful fear of loving child for honored father ...
"the fear of God is the beginning of His love" (Ecclus. 25:16) ...

throughout the Old and New Testaments God asks and asks again for love—

"this only take care of with all diligence, that you love the Lord your God" (Jos. 23:11) ...

"thou shalt love the Lord thy God with thy whole heart, and with thy whole soul, and with thy whole strength" (Deut. 6:5) ...

"the fear of the Lord is honour, and glory, and gladness, and a crown of joy" (Ecclus. 1:11) ...

"if you keep My commandments, you shall abide in my love" (John 15:10) ...

have I learned this loving fear of the Lord? ...
if not, I should let Him teach me ...

Dear Jesus, I want to come to You as You invite me and learn from You all I can, for You know everything and know it perfectly. Don't ever let me fear You in the wrong way, for that would be unjust and untrue to You and me. Teach me above all to love You as a child loves its father with a fear that is filled with love, and a love that fears to offend. Then shall holiness be attractive and I shall be happy in serving You.

THERE IS REST AHEAD

And I heard a voice from Heaven, saying to me:
Write: Blessed are the dead, who die in the Lord.
From henceforth now, saith the Spirit, that they
may rest from their labours; for their works follow
them.—Apoc. 14:13. Used as the Epistle in the daily
Mass for the Dead

Write: Blessed are the dead, who die in the Lord—

    because they have the face-to-face vision of God...

    bceause they enjoy the companionship—

        of Christ their Lord and Brother...

        of Mary their Mother and Queen...

        of all the angels and saints...

        of all their loved ones who are saved...

    but to gain this happiness we must die in the Lord—

        with sanctifying grace in our souls...

        with love in our hearts for Him and for our fellow men...

        as members of His Mystical Body here on earth...

From henceforth now, saith the Spirit, that they may
rest from their labours—

    the labor of conquering self...

    the labor of living lovingly with those at home...

    the labor of dealing in a friendly way with all...

    the labor of earning our daily bread...

    the labor of keeping honest in a dishonest world...

    the labor of taking pleasures decently amid much filth...

For their works follow them—

    "come ye blessed of my Father, possess you the kingdom
prepared for you from the foundation of the world"
(Matt. 25:34)—

        "for I was hungry, and you gave Me to eat" (Ibid. 35)...

        "I was thirsty, and you gave Me to drink" (Ibid.)...

        "I was a stranger, and you took Me in: naked, and you
covered Me; sick, and you visited Me" (Ibid. 35:36)...

"I was in prison, and you came to Me" *(Ibid. 36)*...
and all their prayers follow them...
and all their penances and self-restraints...
and all the reception of all the Sacraments...
am *I* so working now to fulfill God's law in every way that
I shall have many works to follow me?...

Dear Jesus, life is never very easy and it gets real hard at
times. So it is good to know that "there is laid up for me a
crown of justice which the Lord, the just Judge, will give to me."
It helps so much to keep my courage up to know that all my
efforts will be rewarded by You eternally in Heaven. I do want
to fight ahead bravely all the time; and if You ever see me
slackening, please bring back vividly to my mind that "there
remaineth a day of rest for the people of God."

THAT SIGN OF THE CROSS

**This sign of the Cross shall be in Heaven; when
the Lord comes for judgment.**—Versicle and Response
at Vespers of the Feast of the Exaltation of the Cross

This sign of the Cross—

which was a sign of shame and disgrace...
until the day Christ died thereon...
which was the worst means of torment invented by man...
until Christ used it to redeem the world...

This sign of the Cross—

that sign wherewith at Baptism we were ushered into the new
life of grace...
that sign with which we all sign ourselves so often...
that sign with which we shall be lowered into the grave...
that sign which is a true test and testimony of our faith...

Shall be in Heaven—

blazoned in glory...
blazoned before angels and men...
then no longer the crude instrument of disgraceful death...

but the standard of God Himself as He comes to the final judging . . .

When the Lord comes for judgment—

"the day of wrath and of woe when the heavens and the earth shall be moved" *(Burial Prayers)* . . .

"when the Son of man shall come in His majesty, and all the angels with Him" *(Matt. 25:31)* . . .

"then shall the King say to them that shall be on His right hand: Come, ye blessed of my Father" *(Ibid. 34)* . . .

and "to them also that shall be on His left hand: Depart from me, you cursed, into everlasting fire" *(Ibid. 41)* . . .

and I shall be on His right hand if in this life I have—
    signed myself reverently with the sign of the Cross . .
    been faithful to His teachings . . .
    carried my own crosses at least decently well . . .
    and learned to love Him crucified . . .

am I so in love with Him today as to be ready for judgment now? . . .

Dear Lord Jesus, daily we pray in the Mass for those "who are gone before us with the sign of faith and rest in the sleep of peace." I want one day to be among those who are daily numbered in the Memento of the Dead. So let me often devoutly sign myself with the sign of the Cross and let me bear my daily crosses well so that when You come in judgment I may stand on Your right—among the saved.

ALWAYS A SONG OF THANKS

O sing unto the Lord a new song; for He hath done marvelous things.—Introt of the Mass for the Circumcision (New Year's Day)—Taken from Ps. 97:1

O sing unto the Lord a new song—
    "the old year is dying—let it die" . . .
    the old month is dying—let it die . . .
    the old day is dying—let it die . . .

let it die—
>> with its unfaithfulness to God's graces ...
>> with its faults and imperfections ...
>> with its sins and rebellions against God ...

with the New Year, and the new month, and the new day, let us sing a new song—
>> of sincere sorrow for all that is wrong in the past ...
>> of firm resolve to use God's graces in the full ...
>> of renewed love which will have us following Our Lord more closely ...
>> of unstinted service for God—
>>> at home ...
>>> at work ...
>>> at play ...

For He hath done marvelous things—

He created the universe by an act of His will ...

He sustains it in existence lest it cease to be ...

He drew me out of nothingness, and prevents my slipping back thereto ...

He gave Adam grace for me, but Adam tossed it aside ...

He has become Man for me to win me grace again ...

He showers this grace upon me daily, hourly, minutely ...

surely I should sing a new song—
>> each month, each week, each day, each hour ...
>> and make each one *His* ...
>> —in every sense, a year, a week, a day, an hour of *the Lord* ...

Dear Lord, no matter what happens to me, no matter what goes wrong, I should be very happy because You have done marvelous things and are always doing marvelous things to and for me. Let me always serve You with a glad heart and with utter, uncounted generosity; with always a new song of thanks in my heart; and let everyone learn from me that one who loves You and serves You is always happy.

LET'S NOT HARDEN OUR HEARTS

Today, if you shall hear His voice, harden not your hearts.—Ps. 94:8. Used as Invitatory at Matins during Passiontide

Today—

> while life is still strong and buoyant within us . . .
> while "a space for penance" is still ours . . .
> especially during Lent—
> > which is a time of more fervent prayer . . .
> > and a season of deep thought . . .
> > and a period of self-discipline and penance . . .

If you shall hear His voice—

> from His side, there really is no "if"—
> > for He continually enlightens our minds . . .
> > and is ever knocking at the door of our hearts . . .
> but from our side—
> > the clamor of the world is loud, and can easily drown out His voice . . .
> > the enticements of pleasures can readily draw us from Him . . .
> > and the myriad cares of life can push Him aside until we forget Him . . .

Harden not your hearts—

> few of us would dare do that deliberately . . .
> but we can do it in effect—
> > by neglecting prayer—
> > > in the morning and evening . . .
> > > before and after meals . . .
> > > at time of Mass . . .
> > > when we might pay a "pop-call" on Our Lord in the Blessed Sacrament . . .
> > by letting His graces slip by unused—
> > > by infrequent attendance at Mass . . .

by going to Confession and Communion seldom...
by ignoring His plea for more penance and self-denial these days...

He is most worthy of our love...
is it not unthinkable that we should harden our hearts?...

Dear Lord Jesus, it *is* quite unthinkable that anyone of us who know Your love should ever harden his heart against Your call. Yet I do. Maybe not in big things but in so many little ways I don't do and won't do what You want me to. The clear proof of that is that if I did follow Your call always, I'd be a great saint today—and I am far, far away from real holiness. I'm sorry for this and I now beg Your grace to be always eager to await Your call, in little as well as big things, and always quick to do what You want.

GRATITUDE FOR REDEMPTION

We adore Thee, O Christ, and we bless Thee. Because by Thy Holy Cross Thou hast redeemed the world.—Versicle and Response from the Stations of the Cross

We adore Thee O Christ—
as God, from all eternity...
as God-Man, from the moment of Incarnation...
as Creator...
as Redeemer...
as King...
as merciful Pardoner of our sins...

We bless Thee—
with our lips...
in our minds...
from our hearts...
fervently...
frequently...
most gratefully...

Because by Thy Holy Cross—

which the Jews demanded for Your death ...
to which You were condemned by Pilate ...
which You carried out to Calvary ...
to which You were nailed ...
whereupon You hung for three hours ...
on which You died in utter agony ...

Thou hast redeemed the world—

all men without exception ...
men of the Old Law and men of the New Law ...
men who knew You, men who never heard of You ...
redeemed them from original sin ...
redeemed them from personal sins ...
redeemed them as You did Your Mother alone, before sin
   ever touched her ...
redeemed them as You did all others, after sin had stained
   them ...
and among all these was I ...
and You died to redeem me individually and personally ...
and I shall "adore and bless" You by striving to apply
   Your redemption more lavishly to my soul ...

Dear Jesus, here at the foot of Your Cross I kneel to adore
You and bless You because in Your mercy You redeemed me
and all men. But words are not enough. I must show You in my
every thought and word and deed that I am making Your
redemption have its effect on my soul and in my life. Adoration
and blessing with my lips alone will never bring me to Heaven,
and if I don't get there, You will have shed Your Precious
Blood in vain. And that simply mustn't be.

HIS PLEDGE OF LIFE

I am the resurrection and the life.—John 11:25

I am—

yesterday ...
today ...

unto the end of time ...
throughout eternity ...

The resurrection—

from the death of the body—

    from which God had freed Adam ...

    but which was brought back to mankind by Adam's sin ...

    from which no one, not even Christ Himself, has escaped ...

    but which Christ conquered, rising triumphant on the third day ...

    "death is swallowed up in victory. O death, where is thy victory? O death, where is thy sting?" *(I Cor. 15:54,55)* ...

    "in whom Christ the hope of a blessed resurrection shines forth for us, that they who are saddened by the certain doom of dying may be comforted by the promise of future immortality" *(Preface of the Mass for the Dead)* ...

from the death of the soul—

    for Adam had lost sanctifying grace for all of us ...

    for Christ suffered, and died, and rose again, to win us back this sanctifying grace ...

    "for as by the disobedience of one man [Adam], many were made sinners, so also by the obedience of one Christ, many shall be made just" *(Rom. 5:19)* ...

    "and of His fullness we all have received, and grace for grace" *(John 1:16)* ...

The life—

"I am come that they may have life, and may have it more abundantly *(John 10:10)* ...

supernatural life here on earth—

    through sanctifying grace ...

    restored or increased through the Sacraments ...

    enlarged by prayer and good works ...

supernatural life in Heaven—
> seeing God face to face . . .
> and sure of His presence for all eternity . . .
> at *home,* in Father's house . . .

Dear Lord, none of us like to think of death and of the grave so dark and so narrow and so cold. You didn't like to think of it either. But in Your goodness You taught us how to think on the resurrection after our death and the life after our resurrection. And you made that resurrection and that life sure for us by Your own Resurrection and by glorious life in Heaven, and by the grace You give us now. Help me then to make use now of every grace You give me so that one day I shall rise and be with You in Heaven for all eternity.

HOW DO WE TREAT HIM?

The Heart of Jesus, wounded out of love of us: Come, let us adore.—Invitatory of Matins for the Feast of the Sacred Heart

The Heart of Jesus—
> beating for us in the manger crib . . .
> trembling with pain for us at the Circumcision . . .
> forcing the blood out in the agonized sweat of Gethsemani . . .
> pierced by the centurion's spear . . .
> grieved by the ingratitude of men . . .
> symbol of His love and mercy . . .

Wounded out of love for us—
> when Bethlehem had no room for Him . . .
> when Herod sought His life . . .
> when His own people repudiated Him . . .
> when Judas betrayed Him . . .
> when Peter denied Him . . .
> in His Agony, Passion, and death . . .
> down through the centuries—
> > as men rejected Him . . .

as men forgot Him . . .
as even good men failed to live up to His law . . .

Come, let us adore—

for His human heart is substantially united to God . . .
and so is worthy of all love and adoration . . .
and there is much, very much coldness and indifference to
make amends for . . .

and our adoration must be—
constant . . .
fervent . . .
in deeds more than in words . . .
the very best that we can give . . .

Dear Sacred Heart of Jesus, how You have suffered for us!
And how You have suffered from us! Having loved us, Your
own, You love us to the end, to the very limit of love. You
Yourself said that no man has greater love than to lay down his
life for his friends. And that is exactly what You did for us.
But I have repaid You but poorly and have pained You much
by my sins. To put it mildly, and I hope not irreverently, that
isn't fair. I'd be ashamed if I treated a human friend that way—
and now I am truly ashamed for treating You so.

HAVING HIS PEACE

**Grace be to you, and peace from God the Father,
and from the Lord Jesus Christ.**—Customary opening
salutation of St. Paul in his Epistles

Grace—

actual grace which passes with the passing action . . .
sanctifying grace which abides in the soul . . .
in our minds, that we may know His law . . .
in our wills, that we may do His law . . .
for our internal actions, that we may be pleasing to Him . . .
for our external actions, that we may lead others to Him . . .

Peace—

the tranquility that comes from order—

order in our minds, by knowing what God wants...

order in our wills, by obedience to His laws...

order in our emotions, by ruling them as He directs...

order in our homes, that they may be as Nazareth...

order in our social life, that we may take our pleasures holily...

order in our civic life, that all may enjoy its benefits aright...

From God the Father—

who is the Giver of all good gifts...

who is more ready to give than we are to receive...

who knows our needs and will meet them, if we ask Him...

And from the Lord Jesus Christ—

who died to win us grace and peace...

who said: "Peace I leave with you, My peace I give unto you" *(John 14:27)*...

who will grant us eternal peace, if only we remain faithful to the end...

Dear Lord, I need Your grace and peace every day of my life and every moment of every day. There is so much turmoil and trouble in the world and so many temptations and disturbances in my own life that I find it hard not to get upset. But you came to give me peace and to save me from sin by Your grace. So please continue to give me Your grace and let me enjoy that peace in my life that You want me always to have.

LORD, HEAR ME!

Out of the depths I have cried to Thee, O Lord: Lord, hear my voice.—Ps. 129:1,2

Out of the depths—

of my great sorrows and crosses...

of the darknesses of my soul in times of trial...

of the humdrum-ness of daily life ...

of the dull routine of colorless occupations ...

of my fear when I have looked at my sins ...

of my discouragement when I have realized my paltry virtues ...

of my contentedness when life seemed very good ...

of my joys when my heart was quite swept away with them ...

I have cried to Thee—

that my sorrows might not turn me away from You ...

that in my darkness I might not lose my way to You ...

that life's routine might not crowd You out ...

that life's joys might not so appeal to me as to make me forget Your law and Your love ...

Lord, hear my voice—

I am weak, and quick to slip and fall ...

I weary too readily of the fight ...

I find pleasures far too enticing at times ...

but You are strong ...

and You are gracious ...

and You love my soul ...

and You died to save that soul ...

—Lord, hear my voice ...

Dear Lord, I am very much a creature of moods: one time lifted high by a passing joy; another time sunk deep by life's troubles or by an overwhelming realization of what a mess I have made of things. Deep in joy or deep in gloom, seldom sailing calmly on the surface—that is very much the story of my life. It is so hard to ride on an even keel! That is why I call out to You so often: "Lord, save me or I perish." You understand; I know You do. For You have always heard my prayer—and You always will.

ETERNAL REST BE THEIRS!

Eternal rest grant unto them, O Lord: and let perpetual light shine upon them.

—Introit of the Requiem Mass

Eternal rest—

after all life's trumoil and strife . . .
after all the interchange of hopes and fears . . .
after all the strivings that so frequently ended in nothing . . .
after all the heartaches and disappointments . . .
after all the petty jealousies and bickerings . . .

Eternal rest—

there is much peace and happiness in this life . . .
yet not for long . . .
but after death—
nothing can interrupt our joy . . .
nothing can ever cut it off . . .
as long as God is God, we shall be *at home with Him* . . .

Grant unto them, O Lord—

for You are merciful and quick to forgive . . .
and You do not remember our sins once we have repented . . .
and You really want us home with You . . .

And let perpetual light shine upon them—

after the shadows and darknesses of this time of probation . . .
after the doubts and difficulties that so frequently beset our minds . . .
after the hesitancies and failures of our wills . . .
after the twilight of faith whereby we now see You, our God, only obscurely . . .

And let perpetual light shine upon them—

the light of the face-to-face vision of God . . .
when we shall see Him as He really is . . .
when we shall enjoy His intimate companionship for ever . . .

and look deep—
>   into the Mind, that planned all creation . . .
>   into the Will, whose mere "let it be" brought all creation
>   out of nothingness . . .
>   into the Justice, that might have refused to allow the
>   Redemption . . .
>   into the Love, which overrules His Justice and brought
>   Him down to earth for us . . .
>   into the Mercy, that so frequently gave us another
>   chance . . .
>   —and that eternal rest and perpetual light will be mine if
>   I learn to love Him and keep His Law out of love . . .

Merciful Lord Jesus, have mercy on all the Holy Souls and bring them soon into Your joyful presence, for which they long so much. They can no longer help themselves but I can help them by my prayers and good works, and You can help them by Your mercy. And don't forget me, dear Lord, when I come to die and don't keep me waiting too long outside of Heaven. And from my side, I'll do my best now to hurry my entrance into Your Presence by a good and holy life and an ever-growing love for You.

MY ANGEL COMPANION

Behold I will send My angel, who shall go before thee, and keep thee in thy journey, and bring thee into the place that I have prepared.—Exod. 23:20. Used in the Epistle of the Feast of the Guardian Angels.

Behold I will send My angel, who shall go before thee—
>   my Guardian Angel has been with me from the first moment
>   of my existence . . .
>   long years before I could take care of myself, he watched
>   over me . . .
>   by day he guided my steps, and by night he stood on
>   guard . . .
>   a sleepless vigil that not even mother and father could keep . . .

Keep thee in thy journey—

life is a journey—

from birth to death . . .

from infancy to childhood to youth to old age . . .

from this time of exile and of probation to our true home with God . . .

my Angel Guardian keeps me wherever I am—

at home, that I may rightly take my share of its joys and sorrows . . .

at work, that I may play the game of life straight . . .

in times of pleasure, that I may enjoy myself thoroughly without soiling my soul with forbidden pleasures . . .

And bring thee into the place that I have prepared—

first of all by leading me into that state of life where God wants me . . .

and when I have duly chosen it, to help me fulfil its duties and sanctify myself thereby . . .

then when life is over to lead me home to God . . .

"May the angels lead thee into the bosom of Abraham" (*Prayers for the Dying*) . . .

"O God . . . command that he be received by Thy holy angels and taken to Paradise, his true country" (*Ibid.*) . . .

"may the angels lead thee into Paradise . . . may the choirs of the angels receive thee" (*Ibid.*) . . .

Heaven lies at the end of the road and I cannot miss it, if only I let my Guardian Angel have his way . . .

Dear Guardian Angel, I don't pay much attention to you and I never have thanked you much for all your care of me these many, many years. That's quite too bad and quite unmannerly; and I am sorry. You have stood for it all and yet have not neglected me one bit. So from my heart I thank you now and tell you that I do appreciate it all. Just keep watching over me, whether I think of you or not, until you get me home to Heaven. Then I shall really thank you through all the eternal years.

WHOLESOME THINKING OF THE DEAD

It is therefore a holy and wholesome thought to pray for the dead, that they may be loosed from sins.—II Mach. 12:46

A holy thought—

because it is in accord with God's desires...
because by it I practice—
the corporal works of mercy—
feeding those who are hungry to have God...
visiting those who are in the prison of purgatory...
the spiritual works of mercy—
comforting the sorrowful who are pained by their detention away from God...
praying for the dead who can no longer help themselves...
because by it I increace the sanctity of my own soul...

A wholesome thought—

wholesome to the souls in purgatory, because it wins Heaven for them...
wholesome to the Blessed in Heaven, because it brings them new companions...
wholesome to me, because it keeps alive in me a dread of sin and a longing for Heaven...

To pray for the dead—

by saying actual prayers for them...
by having Mass said for them...
by offering up my physical and mental trials for them...

That they may be loosed from sins—

the *guilt* of their sins is, of course, forgiven, for they are really sorry for them...
but the temporal punishment remains, which they did not pay off during life...

so they are now purified of all "the remains of sin" so as to be pure enough to enter Heaven...

by my prayers and good works I can hasten that cleansing and speed that entrance into Heaven...

—and they will not forget me when they stand before God's thone...

Dear Lord Jesus, I must be mindful of the Holy Souls and do all I can to speed their homecoming to You. You want them with You and they want to be with You, and I can help both You and them to bring these desires to fulfilment. So I will pray and work and suffer for them and thus do my part in the Communion of Saints.

STANDING ON THE HEIGHTS

Arise, Jerusalem, and stand upon the heights; and see the happiness which will come to thee from thy God.—Based on Baruch 5:5 and 6:36. Communion of the Mass of the Second Sunday of Advent

Arise, Jerusalem—

these words were first addressed by the prophet Baruch to the stricken Jews in the days of Jeremiah...

and now the Church uses them to arouse us, the dwellers in the new Jerusalem...

we are to arise—

from our easygoing ways...

from our petty infidelities...

from our sins of thought and word and deed...

from our forgetfulness of God...

—for we are to prepare our souls for His coming...

And stand upon the heights—

of self-control, gained through increased acts of mortification.

of recollection, gained by more fervent prayer...

of love of our neighbor, shown by many an act of kindliness...

of love of God, evidenced by the careful fulfilment of each
least duty . .

And see the happiness which will come to thee—
happiness in this world—
for we are to live under the law of love . . .
for we are to be blood brothers of the Man-God . . .
for we are to be members of His Mystical Body . . .
for we are to be temples of the Holy Ghost . . .
happiness in the next world—
enjoying the face-to-face vision of God . . .
having the eternal companionship of Jesus . . .
at home, with God, for ever . . .

From thy God—
only God could think of such happiness . . .
only God could give such happiness . . .
—and sheer decency should make us "arise and stand upon
the heights" . . .

Dear Jesus, You are always wanting to come to me and make
me happy. I wish I were half as anxious to have You come as
You are to come. I need You very much and I need to "stand
upon the heights" always so as to keep before me the vision
of the happiness You want me to have now and for ever. When
I lose sight of that vision I grow slack in holy living and fall too
easily into the lesser sins. So give me grace through prayer and
a spirit of nearness of mind to You to "stand upon the heights"
always—and expectantly.

RUNNING TOWARDS HEAVEN

**Forgetting the things that are behind, and stretch-
ing forth myself to those that are before, I press
towards the mark, to the prize of the supernal
vocation of God in Christ Jesus.—Phil. 3:13,14**

Forgetting the things that are behind—
the sorrows and joys of the years that are gone . . .
the difficulties that beset me at home and beyond my home . . .

the sins that have stained my soul, remembering them only to spur myself on...

the virtues that I may have practiced, recalling them only that I may realize how tepid I have been...

And stretching forth myself to those that are before—

every moment of the oncoming years will bring its chance to practice virtue...

every moment of each month will offer an occasion of self-conquest...

every day will bring its joys and sorrows...

every hour must find me nearer God...

I press towards the mark—

the years are slipping away, and there is not much time left...

and there is so much, so very much left to be done...

and so there must be urgency in my avoidance of sins, and eagerness in my practice of virtue...

The prize of the supernal vocation of God in Christ Jesus—

now, this prize is—
union with Christ in His Mystical Body...
increase of sanctifying grace through holy actions...
a large supply of actual grace to avoid sin and to practice virtue...

hereafter, this prize will be—
a plenitude of happiness...
face to face with God...
at *home* with Him...
eternally...

therefore "let us run by patience to the fight proposed to us: looking on Jesus, the author and finisher of faith" *(Heb. 12:1,2)* ...

Dear Jesus, Heaven is at the end of the road of life if only I keep on the right road. You yourself have told me that it is easy to miss my way unless I keep check on myself and work hard always to keep Your law and grow in Your love. So let me learn to love You each day more and more and thus not merely walk but run merrily towards You in Heaven.

NOT I, BUT CHRIST

He must increase, but I must decrease.—John 3:30

He must increase—

    in my *personal* life—

        God must be more in my *thoughts*—

            so that I dwell on the truths of faith more . . .

            so that I think about Him and His ways more . . .

            so that His views grow more and more to be my views . . .

            so that I always have an atmosphere of nearness to God in my mind . . .

        God must be more in my *will*—

            I must keep His commandments better . . .

            I must resign myself more thoroughly to His plans . . .

            I must accept more graciously the hard things He sends me or allows to come my way . . .

    in my *family and social* life—

        so that home and business and pleasure may be modeled according to His will . . .

        so that He may reign in fact, as well as by right, in all our gatherings . . .

        so that His kingdom may come . . .

        so that His will may be done "on earth as it is in heaven" . . .

I must decrease—

    my own self-seeking must grow less and less . . .

    my pride must yield to lowly-mindedness . . .

    my pleasure-eagerness must be tempered . . .

    my uncharitableness must give place to thoughtfulness for others . . .

    my self-sufficiency must give way to trust in Him . . .

He must increase—I must decrease—

for I am His servant . . .
and He is my Master . . .
for I am His creature . . .
and He is my God . . .
for I am His child . . .
and He is my Father . . .

Dear Lord, I want You to take full possession of my heart and to fill every nook and cranny of it. Whatever of self is there and whatever of human love, I want You to catch it up and make it Yours. Let me increasingly become more like You in thought and word and deed, until all selfishness and self-seeking is pushed out and You are there entirely, and not me at all.

REMEMBERING WHENCE AND WHITHER

Remember, man, that thou art dust; and unto dust thou shalt return—Prayer at the Distribution of the Ashes on Ash Wednesday

Remember—

though dust of dead men is all about me, I am most apt not to think that it will ever be my lot . . .

the things of sense attract me, and so I must recall and think upon the higher truths . . .

I am prone to forget unpleasant things, and so I must deliberately remember death . . .

Man—

animals need not think of death, for there is no after life for them . . .

but man must remember—

for his soul is immortal . . .

and even his body will rise again . . .

this life is but the anteroom of eternity . . .

That thou art dust—

of the first man we read: "And the Lord God formed man of the slime of the earth" *(Gen. 2:7)* . . .

and we are all his children "of the earth, earthly *(I Cor. 15:47)* . . .

and of the products of the dust of earth—

we gain our food . . .

and make our clothing . . .

and build our homes . . .

and fashion our means of travel . . .

dust, yes, and, by the dust, supporting and conserving our frail lives . . .

And unto dust thou shalt return—

"it is appointed unto men once to die, and after this the judgment" *(Heb. 9:27)* . . .

and that hour is coming on apace . . .

and is nearer now than when I read the first line above . . .

and none can stay its coming . . .

and when it comes, it will come as a thief in the night . . .

so it were well to be always ready—

by prayer . . .

by holy living . . .

by doing each single job of life well . . .

"Surely I come quickly: Amen. Come, Lord Jesus" *(Apoc. 22:20)* . . .

Dear Lord, death is coming nearer and nearer each single moment and frankly it is not a pleasant thing to think about from a natural viewpoint. But I really must think of it and it will not be so terrifying if I grow to look on it as a coming home to You. So let me remember that I am dust, but dust that one day will be glorified at home with You forever.

I AM PART OF HIM

Ye are the body of Christ, members of member.
—I Cor. 12:27

Ye—

    each and every one who is baptized—

        despite our sins . . .

        despite our frailties . . .

        despite our lukewarmness in good . . .

        Europeans and Americans . . .

        Asiatics and Africans . . .

        Australians and Oceanians . . .

    and those who are not baptized are called to become members
    of this body . . .

The body of Christ—

    not, of course, His physical body . . .

    but His Mystical Body—

        which came into the fulness of existence on Pentecost . . .

        which is "the fulness of His being" . . .

        which is holy with His holiness . . .

        which reaches through time and space . . .

    which is His Church . . .

    without spot or blemish in itself . . .

    though it can be disfigured by the sinful ways of its earthly
        members . . .

Members of member—

    as in the human body, so in Christ's Mystical Body, member
        differs from member—

        some command, others obey . . .

        some are priests, others layfolk . . .

        some are married, others single . . .

        some fully instructed, others with simplest kind of faith . . .

        some beginning their journey, others nearing home . . .

    but each and all are Christ's body . . .

    and thus holy, by calling . . .

as they should be holy in fact..
and holier and holier as life moves on...

Dear Jesus, what a glorious thing to know that I am part of
You! How proud I should be of that and how it should make
me strain every nerve and sinew to live up to the nobility that
is mine. You are so perfect—yet I am part of You, with all my
imperfections, with all my sins. Aren't You good to put up with
such as me as part of You? But I do want to grow less unworthy
of being one with You. So help me, won't you please?

HIS CROSS BROUGHT HOPE

**But we must glory in the Cross of Our Lord Jesus
Christ; in whom is our salvation, life, and resurrec-
tion; through whom we have been saved and freed.**
—Introt of the Mass for Holy Thursday

But we must glory—

> We—
>> who have been baptized into His Church...
>> who have been called to close intimacy with Christ...
>> who know His love...

> Glory—
>> our boast is not in health, or wealth, or power, or
>> learning...
>> "for the fashion of this world passeth away" (I Cor.
>> 7:31)...
>> our only boast must be that we are followers of the
>> Crucified Christ...

In the Cross of Our Lord Jesus Christ—

> in His own humiliations, Passion, and death...
> for it is we "before whose eyes Jesus Christ hath been set
> forth, crucified among you" (Gal. 3:1)...
> but we must glory too in "the chips from His Cross"—
>> the bodily sufferings that come our way...
>> the anxieties of mind that torture us at times...

the slights and humiliations that are handed out to us . . .
for thereby "I bear the marks of the Lord Jesus in my
body" *(Gal. 6:17)* . . .
and thereby I "fill up those things that are wanting of the
sufferings of Christ, in my flesh" *(Col. 1:24)* . . .

In whom is our salvation, life, and resurrection—

salvation and freedom from sin, and strength to conquer
temptations . . .
life through sanctifying grace now, and in Heaven through
the Beatific Vision . . .
resurrection, now from sin and earthly sordidness, and hereafter from the tomb unto everlasting happiness . . .

Through whom we have been saved and freed—

were it not for Christ's Passion we should still be enslaved
by sin . . .
and we should still be without hope, as the pagans were and
are . . .
"we adore Thee, O Christ, and we bless Thee, because by Thy
holy Cross Thou hast redeemed the world" . . .
—and we must live so as to be worthy of that salvation, life,
and resurrection . . .

Dear Jesus, Your death and Resurrection mean everything to
me. Without them I should be without hope both in this life and
the next, because Adam's sin had shut Heaven's gates against
me. But You have opened them and I may enter in if only I use
Your grace properly. Help me to, won't you?

MAY GOD DISPOSE OUR DAYS

**May almighty God dispose our days and actions in
His peace.**—The Daily Benediction at Prime

Our days—

when the sun is up and we are about our work . . .
when evening falls and we are with our loved ones . . .
when night closes "tired eyelids on tired eyes" . . .

the days of our youth, when life dances merrily along . . .

the days of our maturity, when the weight of life lies full upon us . . .

the days when our steps near the grave, that they may wend homeward . . .

Our actions—

when we pray . . .

when we work . . .

when we play . . .

when we are alone . . .

when we are with others . . .

our inner acts of thought and will . . .

our outer acts of word and listening and deed . . .

May almighty God dispose in His peace—

for He alone can give the peace that is not of this world . . .

peace of mind and heart within us . . .

peace within our home . . .

peace with all our neighbors and fellows . . .

peace with and among all nations . . .

peace founded on His love and His Fatherhood of all . . .

peace here, in this valley of tears . .

peace hereafter, with Him for ever, *at home* . . .

O my God, life here below is a constant struggle and so often the struggle turns into a strife. It is so easy for me to get upset and disturbed and troubled. That does not help me spiritually, and it does not help my love of You. So I ask You, the God of peace, in Your mercy to dispose all my days and actions in Your peace, that peace which the world cannot give and cannot take away.

CATCH ON FIRE WITH HIS LOVE

I am come to cast fire on the earth: and what will I, but that it be kindled?—Luke 12:49

I am come—

down from Heaven where I had been for all eternity . . .

upon this earth in the form of a little Child . . .

and lived as a Man of toil ...
and died as the Man of Sorrows ...
and I came to win men back to God ...

To cast fire on the earth—

the fire of hatred of sin ...
the fire of desire for Good ...
the fire of the love of God ...
fire to purge out all that was base and low and lowering ...
fire to drive men on to loftiest heights of virtue ...

And what will I, but that it be kindled?—

the whole purpose of My existence was to save mankind ...
but men's souls are to be saved by men's cooperation with
My grace ...
and so this fire must be enkindled in each man's heart—
to save his own soul ...
to save other men's souls ...
to drive each man on to spread My kingdom on earth ...
to make them all want to come *home* to Me in Heaven ...

Dear Lord Jesus, I want to catch on fire with Your love and
with a desire to grow in Your love and to make all men know
and love You more. You have deigned to need my help to save
my soul and to save the souls of others. It is through me that
the merits of Your sufferings must be applied to our souls. I am
sorry that I have been so lazy and indifferent in the past. In the
future I shall try to do my best to enkindle and to fan into
flame the fire of Your love in all hearts, my own especially.

ON OUR GUARD

**Wherefore, dearly beloved, waiting for these
things, be diligent that you may be found before
Him unspotted and blameless in peace.**—II Pet. 3:14
Wherefore, dearly beloved, waiting for these things—

for the day when He shall call us *home* ...
for the day when there shall be "new heavens and a new
earth, according to His promises" *(II Pet. 3:13)* ...

for our entrance into Heaven . . .

all this we must keep in mind lest "deceit beguile our soul" (*Wis. 4:11*) . . .

Be diligent—

"with fear and trembling" we must work out our salvation (*Phil. 2:12*) . . .

for we must be on our guard against "the wickedness and the snares of the devil" . . .

Our Lord has died to save us, but we must do our share, too . . .

That you may be found before Him unspotted and blameless—

for "blessed are the clean of heart; for they shall see God" (*Matt. 5:8*) . . .

for every sin—

weakens our love of God . . .

and delays our entry into Heaven . . .

and lessens our merit for all eternity . . .

for we must be perfect as our Heavenly Father is perfect . . .

In peace—

with all men—

for we try not to offend them . . .

and strive to help them if and as we can . . .

with ourselves—

holding our lower natures in proper control . . .

being content with our lot in life . . .

with God—

keeping His commandments . . .

resigning ourselves to His disposal of our lives . . .

loving Him with our whole soul and mind and will and strength . . .

Dear Lord, I must wait for Heaven but while waiting I must be busy about the things You want me to do. It's easy enough to dream about Heaven. It's not so easy to keep working for Heaven all the time. But that is just what I must do. I haven't done it so well in the past, but with Your grace the future will be different.

SEEING AS HE SEES

Lord Jesus Christ . . . grant in Thy mercy that as these lights kindled with visible fire dispel the darkness of night, so our hearts, lighted by invisible fire which is the radiance of the Holy Spirit, may be free from the blindness of sin, and that the eye of our mind being purified we may be able to discern what is pleasing to Thee and profitable to our salvation; so that after the perilous darkness of this life we may deserve to attain the light that fails not.—From the Third Prayer for the Blessing of the Candles on the Feast of the Purification

Lord Jesus Christ . . . grant in Thy mercy that as these lights kindled with visible fire dispel the darkness of night—

rarely do we appreciate what a gift fire is and the light therefrom . . .

the ancients thought it such a gift that they invented the story of Prometheus stealing it from the gods . . .

the "dim-outs" and the "black-outs" of recent years have made us more conscious, if not more grateful of the gift . . .

and we are all praying that soon "the lights go on again all over the world" . . .

So our hearts lighted by invisible fire which is the radiance of the Holy Ghost—

"Come, Holy Ghost, fill the hearts of Thy faithful, and kindle in them the fire of Thy love" (Veni, Sancte Spiritus) . . .

"Come, Holy Ghost, and send from Heaven a ray of Thy light" (Ibid.) . . .

"Come, Light of hearts . . . O most blessed light and fill to the full the hearts of Thy faithful" (Ibid.) . . .

• 142 •

May be free from the blindness of sin—

   sin blinds us naturally by heightening the allure of sinful things . . .

   sin blinds us supernaturally because without sanctifying grace we cannot see God . . .

That our minds being purified we may be able to discern what is pleasing to Thee and profitable to salvation—

   with sin gone, we see all things in right focus . . .

   with sin gone, we see all things with the eyes of God . . .

   with sin gone, Heaven is very attractive . . .

So that after the perilous darkness of this life, we may deserve to attain to the light that fails not—

   it does grow very dark at times in this "valley of tears" . . .

   and we are indeed like those "who sit in darkness, and in the shadow of death" *(Luke 1:79)* . . .

   but God is with us and "if God be for us, who is against us?" *(Rom. 8:31)* . . .

   And life has no perils and death has no fears for us . . .

   placing our trust in God we know that one day we shall be at *home* with Him . . .

   and so to "the King of Kings, and Lord of lords, who alone hath immortality, and inhabiteth light inaccessible . . . be honor and empire everlasting" *(I Tim. 8:15,16)* . . .

(For our closing chat with God we may use the Fifth Prayer of the Candle Blessing.)

O Lord Jesus Christ, You appeared on this day among men in the substance of our flesh, and were presented by Your parents in the Temple. The venerable old man Simeon enlightened by the light of Your spirit, recognized You, took You into his arms and blessed You. Grant us then in Your mercy that enlightened and taught by the grace of the same Holy Spirit we may truly acknowledge You and love You faithfully, who with God the Father in unity with the Holy Spirit, livest and reignest God world without end. Amen.

WALK IN LOVE

Be ye therefore followers of God, as most dear children; and walk in love.—Eph. 5:1,2

Be ye therefore followers of God—

each one of us has an ideal, consciously or unconsciously formed, on which we model our lives . . .

it were well to check often and to find out definitely what is the ideal, that "would-be self," to which I instinctively turn . . .

Our Lord Himself told us: "Be ye therefore perfect, as also your Heavenly Father is perfect" *(Matt. 5:48)* . . .

God having within Himself all that is good is the infinitely perfect ideal on which to model our lives . .

Be ye therefore followers of God—

in His merciful kindness . . .

in His patience . . .

in His understanding tolerance . . .

in His love . . .

As most dear children—

not because He has the power to punish us . . .

not because He knows each thing we do . . .

but because we love Him . . .

and we want to grow more and more like such a devoted Father . . .

And walk in love—

love of God—

which makes us seek every opportunity of fulfilling His will . . .

which makes us grateful for all He has given us: earth and air and sky and sea . . .

which makes us use all things as precious gifts from Him . . .

love of our neighbor—

> because each is a soul redeemed by Him ...
> because each is destined for Heaven like ourselves ...
> because all fundamentally want God even though they
> may be actually far away from Him ...

And walk in love—

> then we shall be happy serving God ...
> then all wrong-doing, great or small, will seem simply out of
> the question for us ...
> then the restraints God put upon us will be seen as proofs
> of His protection ...
> then we shall run merrily on our road home to Heaven ...

Dear Jesus, I want You to be my ideal, the one I "dream about," the one on whom I instinctively mould my life. Any other ideal would be unworthy of me, a soul redeemed by Your Precious Blood. And I want this moulding to be done out of love for You and not because I fear You. You *love* me. Why should I not *love* You in return!

IS CHRIST STILL OUTSIDE THE GATE?

Wherefore Jesus also, that He might sanctify the people by His own blood, suffered outside the gate.—Heb. 13:12

Jesus—

> who is both God and Man ...
> who became Man because of His great love for me ...
> who became Man just to save me ...
> who is my Mother Mary's Son ...
> who is my own Brother ...

That He might sanctify the people—

> all of us, following Adam, had gone far away from God ...
> and we had soiled our souls with many sins ...
> but Christ came to purify us—

our minds—
> from sinful thoughts . . .
> from idle thoughts . . .
> from silly, low ideals . . .

our hearts—
> from love of what is wrong . . .
> from selfishness . . .
> that they might be fit for Him to dwell therein . . .

By His own blood—

our Lord did not merely live for us and set us an example of holiness . . .

but He died for us by one of the most cruel forms of torture ever invented by man . . .

"Greater love than this no man hath, that a man lay down his life for his friends" *(John 15:13)*

and we were not even His friends when He died for us . . .

truly we "are bought with a great price" *(1 Cor. 6:20)*, "with the precious blood of Christ" *(1 Pet. 1:19)* . . .

Suffered outside the gate—

outside the actual gate of Jerusalem, as all criminals did . . .

outside the gate of men's hearts—
> for the Jews rejected Him . . .
> and most men did not know Him . . .

and is He today "outside the gate"—
> of my mind? . . .
> of my memory? . . .
> of my will? . . .

or is He a welcome visitor within the innermost recesses of my soul which He has redeemed? . . .

Dear Jesus, my soul must be very valuable if You purchased it at such a high price. Sometimes when I am thoughtless, I don't think it is so valuable. But You know better than I. So let me always and everywhere realize the value of my soul, and that it belongs to You. You bought it. Thank You for buying it. Don't let me ever steal it from You.